Honda N360, N600, Z 1967-74 Autobook

By Kenneth Ball

Associate Member, Guild of Motoring Writers
and the Autobooks Team of Technical Writers

Honda N360 1967-70
Honda N600 1967-74
Honda Z Coupé 1972-74

Autobooks

Autobooks Ltd. Golden Lane Brighton BN1 2QJ England

The AUTOBOOK series of Workshop Manuals is the largest in the world and covers the majority of British and Continental motor cars, as well as the majority of Japanese and Australian models.

Whilst every care has been taken to ensure correctness of information it is obviously not possible to guarantee complete freedom from errors or omissions or to accept liability arising from such errors or omissions.

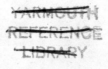

CONTENTS

Acknowledgement

Introduction

ISBN 0 85147 452 7

First Edition   1977

© Autobooks Ltd 1977

743

Printed in Brighton England for Autobooks Ltd by G. Beard and Son Ltd
Bound in Hove England for Autobooks Ltd by Jilks Ltd

A

ACKNOWLEDGEMENT

My thanks are due to Honda for their unstinted co-operation and also for supplying data and illustrations.

Considerable assistance has also been given by owners, who have discussed their cars in detail, and I would like to express my gratitude for this invaluable advice and help.

Kenneth Ball
Associate Member, Guild of Motoring Writers
Ditchling Sussex England.

INTRODUCTION

This do-it-yourself Workshop Manual has been specially written for the owner who wishes to maintain his vehicle in first class condition and to carry out the bulk of his own servicing and repairs. Considerable savings on garage charges can be made, and one can drive in safety and confidence knowing the work has been done properly.

Comprehensive step-by-step instructions and illustrations are given on most dismantling, overhauling and assembling operations. Certain assemblies require the use of expensive special tools, the purchase of which would be unjustified. In these cases information is included but the reader is recommended to hand the unit to the agent for attention.

Throughout the Manual hints and tips are included which will be found invaluable, and there is an easy to follow fault diagnosis at the end of each chapter.

Whilst every care has been taken to ensure correctness of information it is obviously not possible to guarantee complete freedom from errors or omissions or to accept liability arising from such errors or omissions.

Instructions may refer to the righthand or lefthand sides of the vehicle or the components. These are the same as the righthand or lefthand of an observer standing behind the vehicle and looking forward.

CHAPTER 1

THE ENGINE

1 : 1 Description

The 354cc and 598cc engines, fitted to 360 and 600 models respectively, are similar in design and construction apart from minor specification details which will be found in **Technical Data** in the **Appendix**.

The engine is a high performance, transverse two-cylinder unit mated to the transmission and final drive assembly. Primary drive from the engine to the transmission is by means of a roller chain, duplex on manual transmission models, single on automatic transmission models.

The valves are actuated by rocker arms operated from the single overhead camshaft. The camshaft is chain driven from a sprocket on the centre of the crankshaft, the drive passing between the two cylinders. The finned aluminium-alloy cylinders are provided with cast iron liners. The pistons are fitted with two compression and one oil control rings and are fitted with fully-floating gudgeon pins retained by circlips.

The forged steel crankshaft is carried on four needle roller main bearings, similar bearings being used at the connecting rod big-ends. The crankshaft, connecting rods and bearings are factory assembled as an integral unit and must be renewed complete if any part is worn or damaged.

Oil is pressure-fed to the main lubrication points in the engine by a piston-type oil pump mounted in the bottom of the crankcase. Filtration is provided by a renewable cartridge-type filter unit.

The majority of servicing jobs which the owner may wish to do for himself can be carried out with the engine in position in the car. These operations include cylinder head and valve gear removal and servicing of the pistons and cylinders. Engine removal is necessary if the crankshaft and related components are to be overhauled. However, on models fitted with automatic transmission, crankshaft component servicing dictates removal of major parts of the transmission system, this being a specialist job as described in **Chapter 7, Section 7:2**.

FIGS 1:1 and **1:2** show sections through the engine assembly, **FIGS 1:3** and **1:4** show the components of the 360 and 600 units.

1 : 2 Removing the power unit

Before removing the assembly on cars fitted with automatic transmission, reference should be made to **Chapter 7, Section 7:2** for details of the additional procedures to be carried out.

1 Remove the engine crankcase drain plug shown in **FIG 1:5** and drain off the oil, collecting it in a suitable

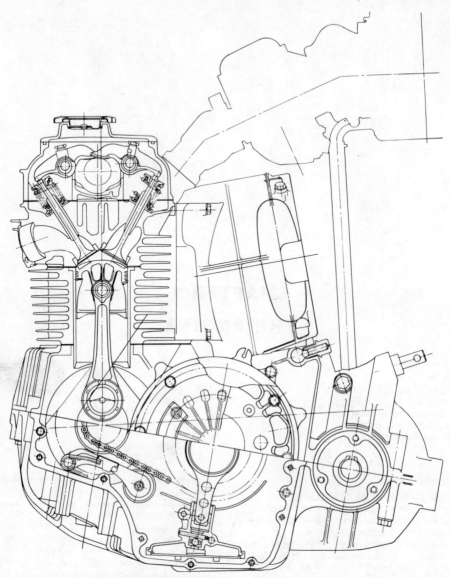

FIG 1:1 Engine cross-section through the centre of a cylinder

container. Disconnect the battery. Remove the exhaust-type heater, if fitted, as described in **Chapter 13**.

2 Refer to **FIG 1:6**, which shows the items to be disconnected. These are the engine ground wire 9, ignition primary lead 11, HT cables 10 and 13, fuel solenoid valve lead 5, back-up (reversing) light cable 2, generator cable and starter cable. Disconnect the clutch cable 6 as described in **Chapter 5**. Disconnect the speedometer, throttle and choke cables.

3 Separate the vacuum tube 3 from the vacuum unit and the breather tube 1 from the camshaft housing

cover. Loosen the clamp 4 and separate the bellows from the air cleaner assembly. Detach the fuel feed pipe from the carburetter.

4 Remove the two insulator mounting bolts arrowed and remove the insulator 12, carburetter and bellows from the camshaft housing as a unit. Take care not to lose the 'O' ring located between the housing and insulator.

5 On cars fitted with engine-type heater units, loosen the hot air duct clamps and separate them from the fan housing. Pull out the heater control rod joint pin to disconnect the rod, then force the rod towards the car interior, as described in **Chapter 13**.

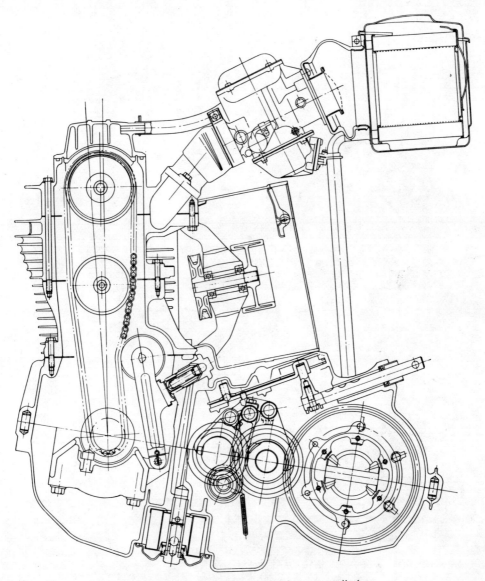

FIG 1:2 Engine cross-section between cylinders

6 Using the special driver or other suitable tool, drive out the joint pin shown in **FIG 1:7** and separate the gearshift column from the rod. Retract the gearshift rod towards the engine, as shown in **FIG 1:8**.

7 Disconnect the wiring for the right and left turn signal lights, at the connectors shown in **FIG 1:9**, bottom arrow.

8 **On 360 models**, remove the front grille and grille screen by taking out the five mounting bolts. **On 600 models**, remove the turn signal light lenses and the bolts attaching the front grille on both sides, then the three screws at the top of the grille. Remove the front grille.

9 Loosen the exhaust clamp nut and release the clamp by removing the bolt securing it to the engine mounting beam, as shown in **FIG 1:10**. Disconnect the exhaust pipe from the cylinder head.

10 Loosen the front wheel nuts and the wheel bearing nuts. Raise the front of the car and support safely on floor stands placed beneath the front body side rails. The supports must be high enough to ensure that the distance between the front bumper and the ground is at least 730mm (28.7in).

11 Remove both wheels and both wheel bearing nuts. Remove the brake drums as described in **Chapter 11**, then separate the brake backplates by removing the

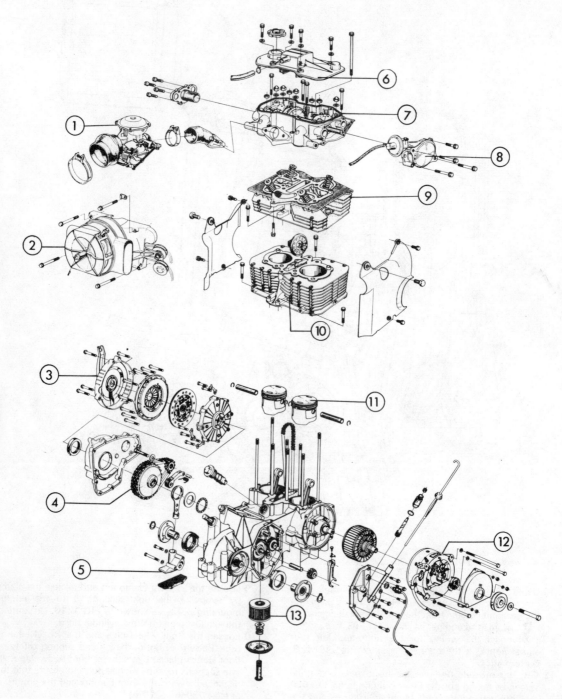

FIG 1:3 Components of the 360 engine

Key to Fig 1:3 1 Carburetter   2 Cooling system   3 Clutch   4 Primary drive   5 Oil pump   6 Camshaft cover   7 Camshaft and housing   8 Contact breaker   9 Cylinder head   10 Cylinder barrel   11 Pistons   12 Generator   13 Oil filter

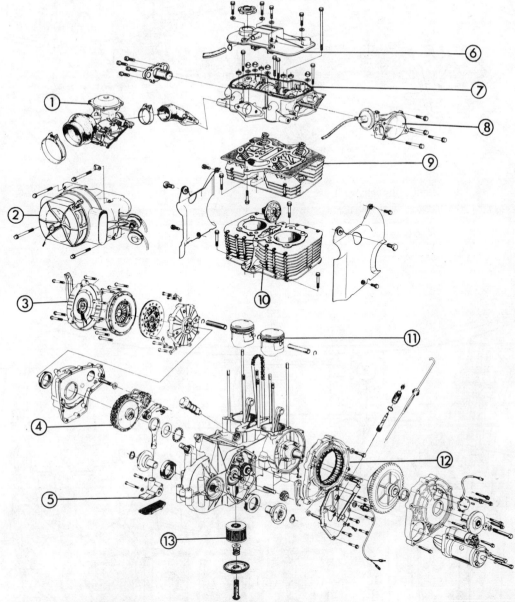

FIG 1:4 Components of the 600 engine

Key to Fig 1:4   See key to **Fig 1:3**

four bolts on each side. Hang the backplates out of the way without straining the brake hoses. Do not disconnect the brake hoses, so that brake system bleeding will not be necessary.

12 Remove the knuckle clamp bolt 2 shown in **FIG 1:11** and separate the knuckle from the damper 3. If difficulty is experienced, insert a screwdriver into the clamp opening and lever carefully.

13 On cars fitted with engine-type heater units, remove the right and left splash guards 1 as described in **Chapter 13**.

14 Remove the front and rear subframe mounting bolts which are shown arrowed in **FIGS 1:12** and **1:13**, making sure that the engine is securely supported on the jack. Remove the two bolts retaining the exhaust silencer to the car body and remove the rubber.

15 Slowly lower the engine/transmission/subframe assembly from the car, checking that no wires or hoses are still connected. Lower the assembly fully and remove from beneath the front of the car.

16 Remove the starter from 600 models. Remove the

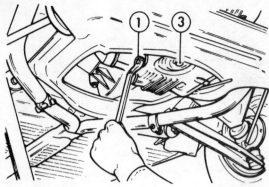

FIG 1:5   Draining the engine oil

Key to Fig 1:5   1 Drain plug   3 Oil filter bolt

FIG 1:7   Disconnecting the gearshift rod

Key to Fig 1:7   1 Punch

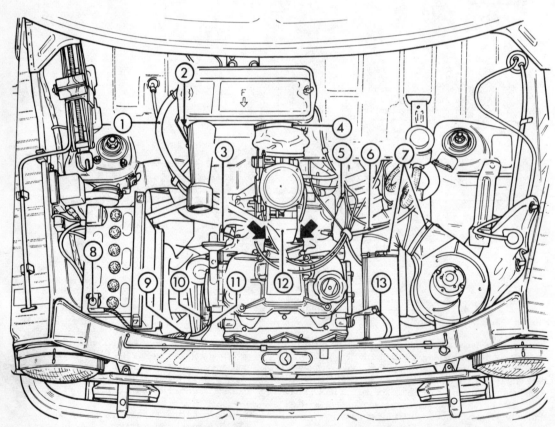

FIG 1:6   Items to be disconnected before engine removal

Key to Fig 1:6   1 Breather tube   2 Reversing light cable   3 Vacuum tube   4 Clamp   5 Fuel solenoid valve lead   6 Clutch cable   7 Heater unit clamps   8 Negative connection   9 Ground wire   10 HT cable   11 Primary lead   12 Insulator   13 HT cable

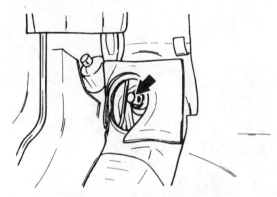

FIG 1:8 Retracting the gearshift rod

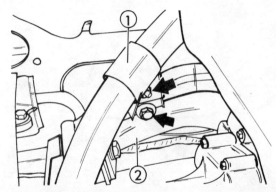

FIG 1:10 Releasing the exhaust pipe clamp 1 from engine mounting beam 2

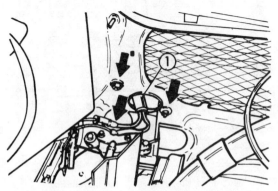

FIG 1:9 Disconnecting the turn signal lights 1

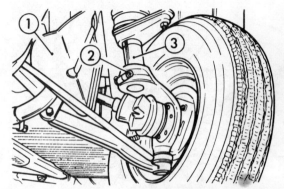

FIG 1:11 Detaching the knuckle from the damper 3. 1 is the splash guard, 2 is the clamp bolt

exhaust pipe and the drive shafts, **FIG 1:14** showing the mounting points of these parts. Remove the four attaching bolts to separate the mounting beam from the engine.

Refitting:

Refitting the assembly to the car is a reversal of the removal procedure, noting the following points:

Make sure that the engine mounting rubber cushions are in good condition. Renew them, if they are worn or perished. The correct assembly of the cushions is shown in **FIGS 1:15** and **1:16**.

When installing the insulator, make sure that the rubber 'O' ring is in position, as shown in **FIG 1:17**.

On completion, check the oil level and adjust the valve clearances, ignition settings and carburetter settings as necessary. Check the front wheel track setting as described in **Chapter 10**.

1:3 Camshaft drive

FIG 1:18 shows the layout of the camshaft drive components. The cam chain tensioner is a hydraulic mechanism which is operated by oil pressure to exert a

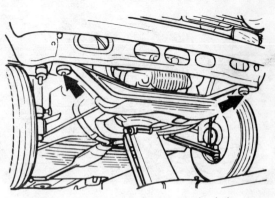

FIG 1:12 Subframe front mounting bolts

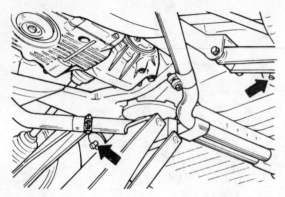

FIG 1:13　Subframe rear mounting bolts

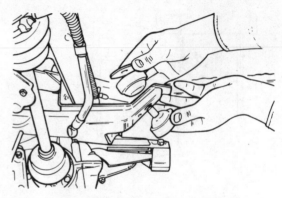

FIG 1:16　Rear mounting rubber installation

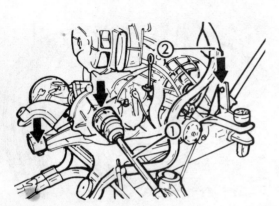

FIG 1:14　Removing the exhaust pipe 2 and the drive shafts 1

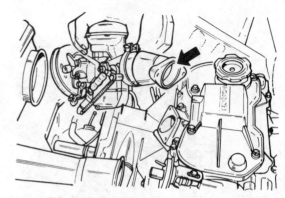

FIG 1:17　Insulator 'O' ring installation

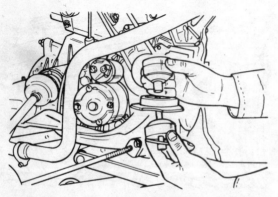

FIG 1:15　Front mounting rubber installation

tightening force on the chain. This prevents chain jumping and reduces operational noise. If excessive chain noise or mechanical engine noise around the region of the cylinders is noticed, the chain tensioner should be examined. If the tensioner fails and the engine is kept running, the chain will damage the cylinder head and barrel.

Chain tensioner removal:

The chain tensioner location is shown in **FIG 1:19**. Use the correct size socket spanner to unscrew the unit, not an open-ended spanner. If the unit is stiff, tap against the hexagon with a plastic hammer to free the threads.

Servicing:

Test the tensioner by holding in a pan of clean engine oil, as shown in **FIG 1:20**. Depress the pushrod several times to fill the unit with oil. If, when the unit is filled with oil, the pushrod can be depressed in a short time, the check valve is faulty.

To renew the check valve and pushrod holder, which form a sealed assembly, use a valve spring compressor or similar means to dismantle the unit, as shown in

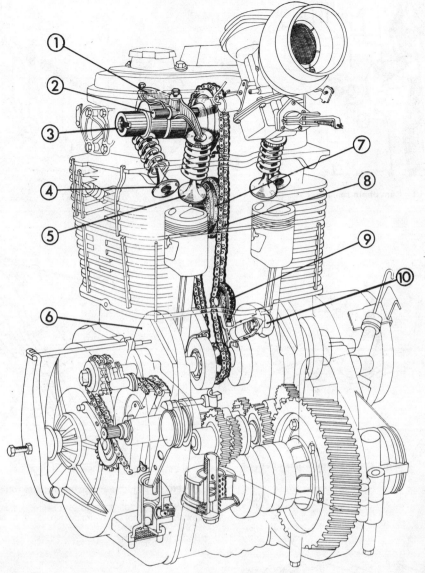

FIG 1:18   Camshaft drive components

Key to Fig 1:18   1 Rocker arm   2 Rocker arm shaft   3 Camshaft   4 Exhaust valve   5 Inlet valve   6 Crankshaft   7 Chain guide roller   8 Camshaft drive chain   9 Chain tensioner roller   10 Chain tensioner

FIG 1:21. A bolt or similar should be fitted between the tool and the pushrod, then the tool compressed enough to allow the removal of the retaining clip with a screw driver. This done, release the tool and remove the internal components, as shown in **FIG 1:22**. Discard the old check valve and pushrod holder and check the remaining components, renewing any found worn or damaged. Reassemble in the reverse order of dismantling, using a new check valve and pushrod holder. Refit the tensioner assembly to the engine, then run the engine to check the operation.

Tensioner guide roller:

The tensioner guide roller assembly consists of a synthetic rubber roller, a rubber cushion against which the pushrod operates and the arm which pivots on a mounting on the crankshaft centre bearing cap, as shown in **FIG 1:23**. The unit can be inspected for wear when the cylinders are removed, but the crankcase must be dismantled before the unit can be removed. During inspection, the rubber roller should be checked for wear or damage and the rubber pad for security and good condition.

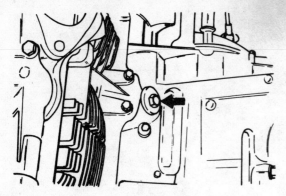

FIG 1:19   Cam chain tensioner removal

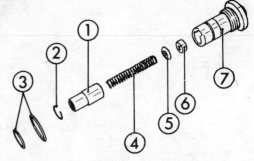

FIG 1:22   Chain tensioner components

Key to Fig 1:22 1 Pushrod 2 Clip 3 'O' rings 4 Spring 5 Spring seat 6 Check valve 7 Pushrod holder

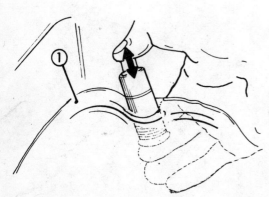

FIG 1:20   Testing the cam chain tensioner

Key to Fig 1:20 1 Clean engine oil

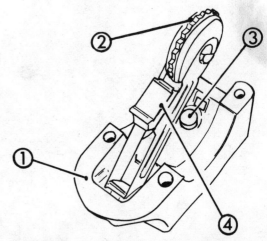

FIG 1:23   Chain tensioner guide roller assembly

Key to Fig 1:23 1 Crankshaft centre bearing cap 2 Guide roller 3 Cam chain stopper pin 4 Rubber cushion pad

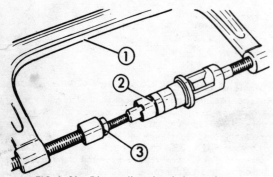

FIG 1:21   Dismantling the chain tensioner

Key to Fig 1:21 1 Valve lifter 2 Pushrod holder assembly 3 6mm bolt

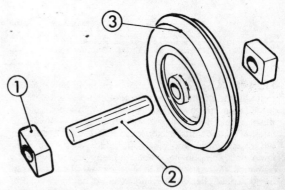

FIG 1:24   Upper chain guide roller 3, rubber bushings 1 and spindle 2

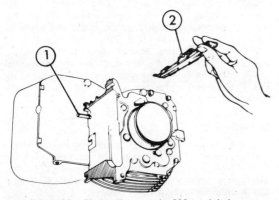

FIG 1:25   Chain slipper unit, 600 model shown

Key to Fig 1:25   1 Long pin   2 Short pin

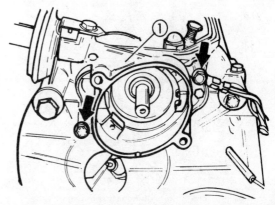

FIG 1:26   Removing the right camshaft holder 1

Upper guide roller and chain slippers:

The upper guide roller is located at the mounting surface (see **FIG 1:18**) between the cylinder barrels and cylinder head. **FIG 1:24** shows the components. During servicing, the roller should be checked for excessive wear at the chain contact face and the rubber bushings checked for good condition, any faulty parts being renewed.

The chain slipper unit is secured to the cylinder barrel by one pin on 360 models, by two pins on 600 models. The location of the unit is shown in **FIG 1:25**. On 600 models, the longer pin fits in the groove of the cylinder barrel at the top, the shorter pin in the centre of the slipper unit. When the engine is dismantled for overhaul, the slipper should be checked for excessive wear, and renewed if necessary.

1:4 Camshaft and rocker shaft servicing

Dismantling:

Remove the carburetter from the engine, together with the inlet manifold. On cars fitted with engine-type heaters, disconnect the control rod and push it towards the car interior, as described in **Chapter 13**. Loosen the air duct clamps and separate the air ducts from the cooling fan housing.

Separate the cooling fan housing from the engine and remove the fan belt from the pulley, as described in **Chapter 4**. Remove the hydraulic cam chain tensioner as described previously.

Remove the camshaft housing cover and remove the right camshaft holder, as shown in **FIG 1:26**. The contact breaker assembly, which is contained within the housing, is covered in **Chapter 3**.

FIG 1:27 shows the removal of the rocker arm shaft. A spring is installed to the inlet rocker arm shaft, while a rubber spacer (or a spring on certain models) is installed on the exhaust rocker arm shaft. On models which are fitted with a spring on each shaft, be sure to note the correct position of the springs for refitting in their original positions. Loosen the rocker arm locking bolts and withdraw the exhaust rocker arm shaft.

Refer to **FIG 1:28** and remove the left camshaft holder, then remove the inlet rocker arm shaft in the

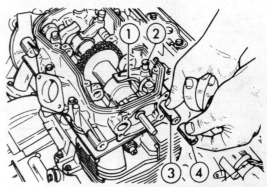

FIG 1:27   Rocker arm shaft removal

Key to Fig 1:27   1 Exhaust rocker arm   2 Locking bolt
3 Rocker arm shaft   4 Distance piece

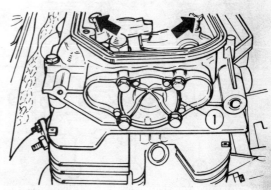

FIG 1:28   Removing the left camshaft holder 1, locking bolts arrowed

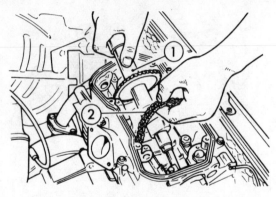

FIG 1:29 Camshaft removal

FIG 1:30 The camshaft housing bolt

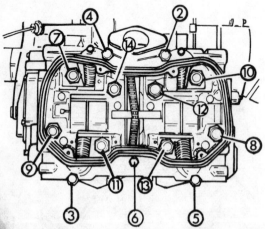

FIG 1:31 The camshaft housing nuts, loosen in the order shown and tighten in the reverse order. On 600 models, cap nuts are in positions 12 and 14 only

same manner as before. Remove the chain 2 from the camshaft sprocket, then pull out the camshaft 1 towards the left side as shown in **FIG 1:29**.

Remove the cooling shrouds from both sides as described in **Chapter 4**. Take out the bolt arrowed in **FIG 1:30**, then loosen the nuts in the order shown in **FIG 1:31**. Remove the nuts and lift off the camshaft housing casting.

Servicing:

Check the inside diameter of the rocker arm shaft bearing bosses in the housing. The housing must be renewed if any outer diameter exceeds 17.05mm (0.671in) or if any inner diameter exceeds 12.05mm (0.474in), these being the wear limits.

Remove the old gaskets and discard them. Check the camshaft housing to cylinder head mating surface and smooth the surface carefully with a fine oilstone if it is pitted or scratched. If there are any signs of oil leakage, the surface should be checked on a surface plate and high spots removed with the stone.

The camshaft should be mounted on V-blocks and rotated, with a dial gauge bearing on the shaft to check for distortion. Renew the camshaft if bending is in excess of 0.04mm (0.0016in). Inspect the cam lobes for wear with a micrometer, measuring from the top of the lobe to the base of the cam. The camshaft should be renewed if any lobe is below the wear limit, the wear limits being as follows:

360 models: inlet cam 39.70mm (1.563in); exhaust cam 40.22mm (1.583in).

600 models: inlet cam 41.18mm (1.621in); exhaust cam 40.70mm (1.602in).

Measure the root diameter of the camshaft sprocket between two diametrically opposite points. Renewal is necessary if the measurement is less than 79.1mm (3.114in). Check the camshaft journal diameter and renew if this is less than 23.9mm (0.941in). The bearing bores in the camshaft journals should not exceed an inside diameter of 24.05mm (0.9468in).

Inspect the rocker arms for wear or scoring on their bearing surfaces and at the points where the tips act on the camshaft and valves. Renew any unserviceable rocker arm.

Assembly:

This is a reversal of the dismantling procedure, using new gaskets throughout and noting the following points:

Refit the camshaft housing with the bolt and nuts finger tight. Note the correct positions of the cap nuts, as shown in **FIG 1:31**. Tighten the nuts a little at a time, in the reverse order to that shown in the illustration, to a final torque of 2.8 to 3.2kgm (20.3 to 23.1lb ft) for the 10mm nuts, 0.9 to 1.2kgm (6.5 to 8.7lb ft) for the 6mm nuts. Tighten the bolt similarly.

Install the camshaft, then turn the engine in the normal rotation direction until the T-mark on the engine crankshaft pulley is exactly aligned with the index mark. Now turn the camshaft until the line on the sprocket is as shown in **FIG 1:32**, at the top and parallel with a straightedge placed across the housing flange surfaces. In this position, pull on both ends of the camshaft chain

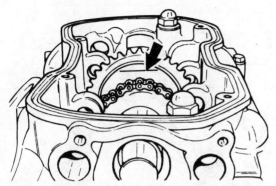

FIG 1:32 Camshaft sprocket timing mark alignment

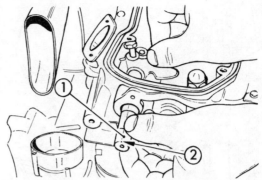

FIG 1:33 Rocker arm shaft 1 installation, 2 is the punch mark

to remove any slack, then mount the chain on the sprocket without disturbing the setting. This operation correctly sets the valve timing.

The rocker arms are marked R and L to denote right and left side components and must be fitted correctly. The camshaft holder for the righthand side must be installed first. Install the rocker arm shafts with the punch mark to the top, as this will provide maximum valve clearance and ease the fitting operation. **FIG 1:33** shows the location of the punch mark 2. Make sure that the springs are correctly refitted in the order noted during dismantling.

Inspect the oil seal in the right side camshaft holder and, if it is worn or damaged, remove it and fit a new seal with special tool 1 or similar, as shown in **FIG 1:34**. Install the right camshaft holder with a new gasket.

Turn the engine crankshaft one complete turn, realigning the crankshaft pulley T mark with the index. Install the left camshaft holder by offsetting it 90° as shown in **FIG 1:35**. In this position, install the rocker arms and shafts, then rotate the camshaft holder to its correct position and tighten the mounting bolts.

Adjust the valve clearances as described in **Section 1:5**.

1:5 Valve clearance adjustment

The correct adjustment of valve clearances is important as it affects engine timing and performance considerably. Excessive clearance will reduce valve lift and opening duration and reduce engine performance, causing excessive wear on the valve gear components and noisy operation. Insufficient or zero clearance will again affect engine timing and, in some circumstances, can hold the valve clear of its seat. This will result in much reduced performance and the possibility of burned valves and seats. Valve clearances should be checked at the recommended service intervals as routine maintenance and, additionally, whenever camshaft or cylinder head servicing has been carried out. Checking should also be carried out whenever valve gear noise is noticed.

The valve clearances must be checked and adjusted when the engine is cold, so allow it to cool down completely before proceeding. The correct clearances are 0.08 to 0.12mm (0.003 to 0.005in) for both inlet and exhaust valves.

Remove the camshaft cover to expose the rockers. Turn the engine until two valves are lifted fully by the camshaft

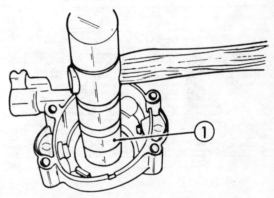

FIG 1:34 Camshaft holder oil seal renewal

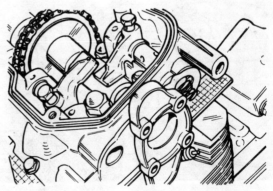

FIG 1:35 Installing the left camshaft holder

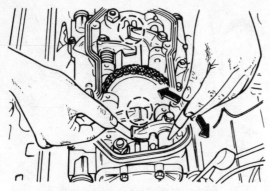

FIG 1:36 Valve clearance adjustment

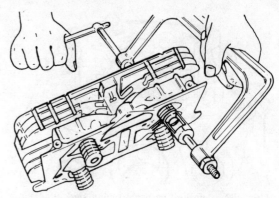

FIG 1:39 Removing the valves from the cylinder head

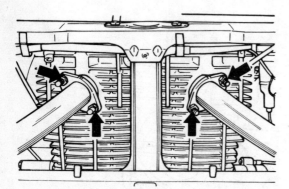

FIG 1:37 Exhaust pipe removal

FIG 1:38 The cylinder head bolt

lobes, as shown in **FIG 1:36**. Now check the clearances at the remaining two valves, using feeler gauges between the rocker tip and the cam lobe. If any clearance is incorrect, loosen the rocker arm locking bolt on the rocker concerned and turn the rocker shaft to adjust the clearance to specification. Use the special tool shown or a suitable metal rod for the purpose. When the clearance is correct, tighten the bolt and recheck the clearance, as it may change during tightening. Turn the engine until the two valves checked are in the fully open position, then check the other two clearances in the manner described. Refit the camshaft cover and run the engine to check for oil leaks.

1:6 Cylinder head and valves

Removal:

Remove the camshaft housing assembly in the manner described previously. Remove the front grille and screen, then detach the exhaust pipes from the cylinder head as shown in **FIG 1:37**. Remove the bolt circled in **FIG 1:38**, then lift the cylinder head from the cylinders. Remove and discard the cylinder head gasket.

Servicing:

Clean the carbon from the combustion chambers before removing the valves, to prevent damage to the valve seats. Do not use sharp tools for this cleaning job as they would damage the light alloy surfaces.

Use a valve spring compressor tool to remove the valves from the cylinder head, as shown in **FIG 1:39**. With the spring compressed, remove the split taper collets then release the tool. Remove the spring, cap and valve, marking the components for correct refitting in their original positions.

Check the cylinder head to cylinder mating surface and smooth the surface carefully with a fine oilstone if it is pitted or scratched. Check the surface with a straightedge or surface plate and remove any high spots with the stone.

Valves:

When the valves have been cleaned of carbon deposits they must be inspected for serviceability. Valves with bent stems or badly burned heads must be renewed. Valves that are pitted can be recut at a service station,

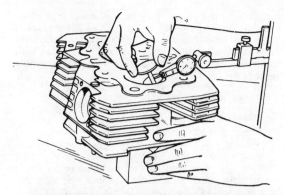

FIG 1:40   Checking valve guides for wear

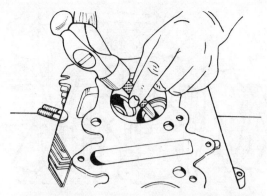

FIG 1:41   Fitting a new valve guide

but if they are too far gone for this treatment, new valves will be required. The correct valve seat angle for all valves is 45°.

Check the diameter of each valve stem at several points. Renew inlet valves if the stems are less than 6.56mm (0.258in) in diameter, exhaust valves if less than 6.53mm (0.257in) diameter.

Valve guides:

Valve guides that are worn or scored must be renewed. Check for wear by inserting the valve into its guide as shown in **FIG 1:40**, then moving the valve to and fro against the gauge stem. The guide should be renewed if the movement exceeds 0.08mm (0.0032in) for inlet valves, 0.11mm (0.0043in) for exhaust valves.

To renew a valve guide, drive out the old guide from the cylinder head and drive in a new one, remembering to re-install the clip, using a suitable punch as shown in **FIG 1:41**.

The new guide should then be reamed to accept the valve stem, new guides being undersize to allow for this procedure. If the guide is not reamed correctly the valve will stick during operation. On completion, the valve seat in the cylinder head should be recut to ensure concentricity.

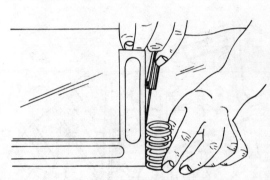

FIG 1:42   Checking a valve spring for distortion

Valve springs:

Test the valve springs for distortion by placing on a surface plate and using a square as shown in **FIG 1:42**. Any spring which is more than 1.5mm (0.06in) out of square should be renewed.

The tension of used springs can be checked by comparing them with a new spring. To do this, place both the old and new spring end to end, with a metal plate between them, into the jaws of a vice. If the old spring is weakened, it will close up first when pressure is applied. Take care that the springs do not fly out of the vice under pressure. Any spring which is shorter or weaker than standard should be renewed.

Refitting:

This is a reversal of the removal procedure, using new gaskets throughout. Make sure that the two hollow pins are correctly installed before fitting the head, as arrowed in **FIG 1:43**. Clean carbon from the piston crowns,

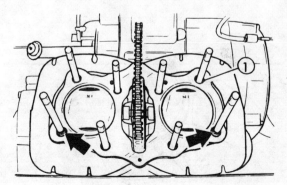

FIG 1:43   Installation of the hollow pins arrowed and gasket 1

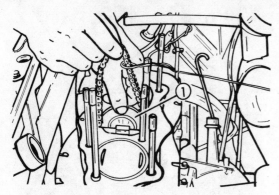

FIG 1:44 Removing the camshaft guide roller 1

FIG 1:45 Piston removal

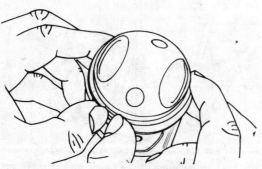

FIG 1:46 Removing piston rings

making sure that no dirt falls down the camshaft chain passage into the crankcase. Do not use sharp tools to clean the pistons and avoid scratching the light-alloy surfaces. Attach a piece of wire or cord to the camshaft chain and use this to pull the chain through the cylinder head as the head is fitted.

1:7 Pistons and cylinders

Removal:

Remove the camshaft housing and the cylinder head assemblies, all as described previously. Remove the camshaft chain guide roller as shown in **FIG 1:44**, hooking a wire or cord around the chain to prevent it from falling into the crankcase. Remove one front and two rear cylinder to crankcase mounting bolts, then gently lift the cylinder assembly from the crankcase. If the cylinder assembly is stuck, use a screwdriver and gently tap all around the cylinder barrels, then gently pry the cylinders from the crankcase. Take great care to avoid damaging the joint surfaces or cooling fins.

Wrap a piece of rag around the connecting rod beneath the piston to prevent anything from falling into the crankcase, then remove the circlip from one side of the piston, as shown in **FIG 1:45**. Push out the gudgeon pin and remove the piston from the connecting rod. Repeat the operation to remove the second piston, keeping all parts in the correct order for refitting in their original positions. Carefully spread the piston rings and remove them from the pistons, as shown in **FIG 1:46**.

Servicing:

Remove all old gasket material from the machined surface of the cylinder barrel assembly, then check the condition of the surface in the manner previously described for the cylinder head.

Cylinders:

Use a dial gauge to check the cylinder bore diameter, the difference between the minimum and maximum diameter and the out of roundness of the bore. The serviceable limits are as follows:

	360	*600*
Cylinder diameter	62.60mm	74.10mm
	(2.4640in)	(2.9173in)
Diametrical	0.01mm	0.05mm
difference	(0.0004in)	(0.0020in)
Out of roundness	0.01mm (0.0004in) to	
(both models)	0.05mm (0.0020in)	

If cylinder wear is beyond the serviceable limit at any point, reboring to accommodate oversize pistons will be necessary, this being a specialist job. Oversize pistons are available in 0.25mm (0.0098in) increments.

Pistons:

Use a micrometer to check the piston diameter at the top land A and skirt B, as shown in **FIG 1:47**. The serviceable limits are as follows:

	360	*600*
Top land diameter	61.95mm	73.40mm
	(2.439in)	(2.890in)
Skirt diameter	62.40mm	73.90mm
	(2.457in)	(2.909in)

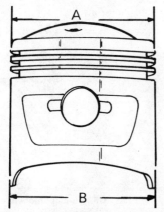

FIG 1:47   Checking piston diameter

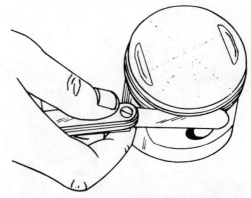

FIG 1:48   Checking piston ring side clearance

If piston wear is beyond the serviceable limit at any point, or if there are signs of scoring or seizure, the piston must be renewed. If the cylinder bore is in good condition, a new piston of the original size may be fitted, otherwise oversize pistons must be fitted after cylinder reboring. If the original pistons are to be re-used, clean off all carbon and lacquer deposits and make sure that the oil holes in the ring groove are clear.

Piston rings:

Fit the piston rings one at a time into the grooves from which they were removed, then check the side clearance between the ring and groove as shown in **FIG 1:48**, using feeler gauges. Do this at four equally spaced points around the piston. Make sure that there is no carbon in the ring groove to affect the measurement. Clean carbon from ring grooves if necessary, using a piece of old piston ring ground to a chisel point or other suitable tool. If the side clearance exceeds 0.105mm (0.004in), the ring, piston or both must be renewed to correct the clearance.

Fit the piston rings one at a time into the cylinder bore from which they were removed, pushing the ring to a point approximately 20mm (0.8in) from the bottom of the bore with the inverted piston to ensure squareness, as shown in **FIG 1:49**. Use feeler gauges 1 to check the gap between the ends of the piston ring 2, which should not exceed 0.6mm (0.023in). If the gap is wider than the stated figure, the ring must be renewed.

Refitting:

This is a reversal of the removal operation, noting the following points:

Install the piston rings carefully to avoid breakage, making sure that the lettered side of each ring is upward. The pistons must be fitted with the side marked 'IN' towards the inlet manifold side of the engine. Check the gudgeon pins before refitting and renew them if they are less than 16.97mm (0.6681in) in diameter at any point. Check the gudgeon pin retaining circlips for a good fit in the piston grooves, renewing any circlip found damaged or distorted.

When installing the cylinder barrel assembly, use flat pieces of wood as piston seats and a suitable set of piston

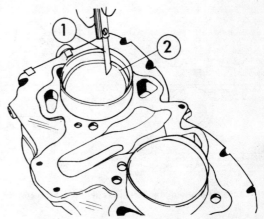

FIG 1:49   Checking piston ring fitted gap

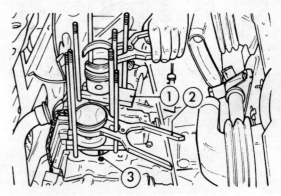

FIG 1:50   Fitting piston seats 1 and piston ring clamps 2 before cylinder installation. 3 is the hollow pin

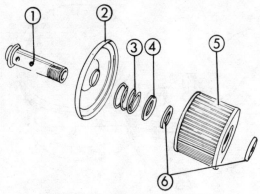

FIG 1:51 Oil filter components

Key to Fig 1:51 1 Oil filter bolt 2 Filter cover 3 Spring 4 Spring seat 5 Element 6 Rubber seals

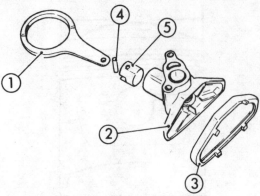

FIG 1:54 Oil pump components

Key to Fig 1:54 1 Pump rod 2 Pump body 3 Strainer 4 Pin 5 Plunger

ring compressors, as shown in **FIG 1:50**. Smear the cylinder bores and piston surfaces with clean engine oil, then carefully lower the cylinder barrel assembly over the pistons. When the rings have entered the bores, remove the clamps and piston seats and push the barrels fully home.

1:8 Lubrication system

Oil filter renewal:

The oil filter element should be renewed after the first 5000km (3000 miles) and every 10,000km (6000 miles) thereafter.

Remove the filter through bolt and remove the filter cover, having a container ready to catch any oil spillage. Remove and discard the old filter element. Fit the new element into position, as shown in **FIG 1:51**, then refit the cover and through bolt. Run the engine and check for oil leaks, then check and top up the engine oil level.

Oil pump:

Removal:

Remove the oil drain plug from the bottom of the crankcase (see **FIG 1:5**) and allow the oil to drain into a suitable container. Remove the clutch assembly as described in **Chapter 5**. Refer to **FIG 1:52** and remove the left side cover from the engine. If the side cover lower bolts are difficult to reach, jack up the engine slightly to improve access.

The oil pump is removed together with the primary drive sprockets and chain as an assembly. Refer to **FIG 1:53**. Remove the driven sprocket circlip and remove the washer 5 from the mainshaft. Remove the drive sprocket retaining bolt 4 and washer 3. Remove the two oil pump retaining bolts arrowed and special washers. Draw out the pump assembly 6 with the primary drive assembly by pulling the two sprockets off their shafts together.

Servicing:

Remove the strainer 3 from the pump 2. Remove the pin 4 and detach the plunger 5 from the pump rod 1, as shown in **FIG 1:54**.

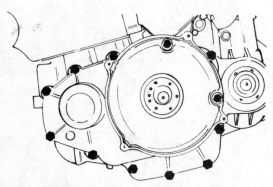

FIG 1:52 Removing the left side cover from the engine

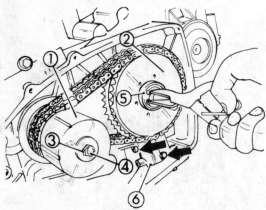

FIG 1:53 Removing the oil pump and primary drive assembly

Key to Fig 1:53 1 Drive sprocket 2 Driven sprocket 3 Washer 4 Bolt 5 Washer 6 Oil pump

Thoroughly clean the strainer in petrol or by washing in a detergent solution. If the strainer will not clean up properly, or if it is damaged, renew it.

Use a dial gauge and micrometer respectively to check the cylinder internal diameter and the plunger outer diameter. Renew the body assembly if cylinder diameter is less than 22.05mm (0.8681in) or if the bore is scored or damaged. Renew the plunger if the diameter is less than 21.91mm (0.8626in) or if it is worn or damaged. If the plunger and cylinder are in good condition but pump operation is faulty, the valves will be defective and the body assembly should be renewed. Check the pump rod thrust needle bearing is in good condition, renewing it if worn, seized or damaged.

Refitting:

Fit the needle roller bearing 3 and thrust plate 2 over the mainshaft 1, as shown in **FIG 1:55**, then reassemble the remaining components in the reverse order of dismantling, noting the following points:

Fit the pump rod to the sprocket with the grooved side of the rod facing the sprocket. Special iron washers are used with the pump installation bolts, always use these and no other type. Install the primary drive and driven sprockets as described in **Section 1:9**. Make sure that the two locating pins are in place in the holes on each side of the crankcase before refitting the left side cover, replacing them with new packing.

1:9 Primary drive

Removal:

Removal of the primary drive chain and sprockets is carried out as described in **Section 1:8**, together with the oil pump assembly.

Servicing:

Check the tension of the primary chain tensioner spring 2, using a spring scale 3 as shown in **FIG 1:56**. The spring must be renewed if tension is less than 1.6kg (3.53lb) for 360 models, 3.6kg (7.92lb) for 600 models. Renew the tensioner roller if it is worn or damaged.

On 600 models, check the side clearance of the drive sprocket with a feeler gauge 1, as shown in **FIG 1:57**. Standard clearance is 0.2mm (0.0078in). Excessive clearance will cause rapid chain wear, so if the clearance is more than the stated figure, check the thrust plate for a thickness of 2.94 to 3.06mm (0.1157 to 0.1204in) and renew it if less. Also check for worn damper rubbers as described later.

Check the side clearance of the primary driven sprocket, using two feeler gauges as shown in **FIG 1:58**. The figure should be between 0.1 and 0.3mm (0.0039 and 0.0118in). Excessive clearance can cause rapid chain wear and leakage through the oil seal, so the sprocket hub and thrust washer should be checked for wear and distortion and defective parts renewed.

Check the primary chains for wear and loose links, renewing the chain if it is defective in any way. Check the driven sprocket for eccentricity and radial play, using a dial gauge. This standard value is 0.3mm (0.0118in). If this is exceeded, the cause may be due to worn sprockets, driven sprocket hub and/or setting plate, or to

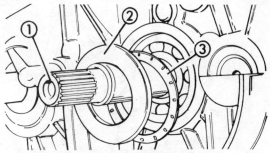

FIG 1:55 Fitting the pump thrust plate 2 and needle bearing 3

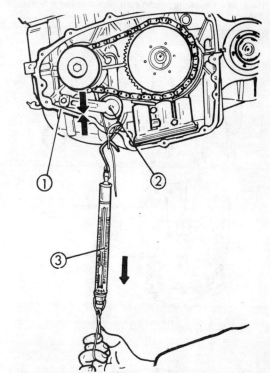

FIG 1:56 Checking primary chain tensioner spring

FIG 1:57 Checking drive sprocket side clearance, 600 models

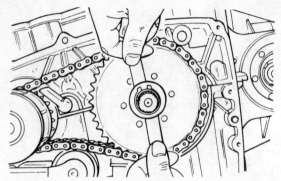

FIG 1:58 Checking primary driven sprocket side clearance

FIG 1:61 Driven sprocket and hub assembly, 1970 600 models

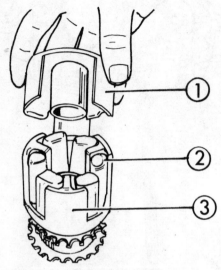

FIG 1:59 Drive sprocket hub assembly

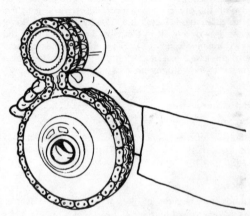

FIG 1:62 Checking the chain fit on the sprockets

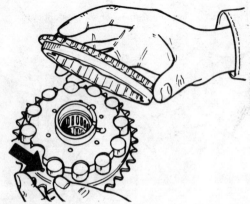

FIG 1:60 Driven sprocket and hub assembly, all but 1970 600 models

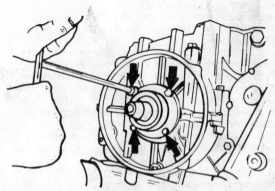

FIG 1:63 The right main bearing holder retaining bolts

a worn sprocket needle bearing. Also check the transmission mainshaft bearing for excessive play by moving the end of the shaft.

Check the damping rubbers in the driven and drive sprockets and renew any rubber which is worn, damaged or distorted.

Reassembly:

In addition to the instructions given here, reference should be made to **Section 1:8** when fitting the oil pump and sprocket assemblies.

Grease the drive sprocket damper rubbers 2 and assemble the sprocket 3 and hub 1 as shown in **FIG 1:59**, compressing the parts in a vice if assembly is difficult.

On 600 models, install one sprocket on the driven sprocket hub and install the damper rubbers, greasing the rubbers if difficult to fit. The rubbers must be fitted with the point mark or the Y-mark upwards, whichever identification is used. When the rubbers are tightly installed, fit the second sprocket as shown in **FIG 1:60**, aligning the punch marks on the inner and outer sprockets. On 1970 600 models only, install the sprockets to the hub so that the aligning mark on the inner sprocket is separated about 180° from the mark on the outer sprocket, as shown in **FIG 1:61**, making sure that the teeth are staggered as shown in the inset.

Fit the set plate to the sprocket hub, with the chamfered side facing the hub. Loop the chains around the sprockets and check their fit by holding the chains and sprockets together and pinching the chains between the sprockets as shown in **FIG 1:62**.

Refit the remaining components in the reverse order of removal, noting the following points:

On 600 models, install the thrust plate with the grooved side outwards before fitting the drive sprocket. Install the sprockets, chains and oil pump assembly as a single unit as described in **Section 1:8**. Tighten the drive sprocket to a torque of 2.5kgm (18lb ft).

1:10 Crankshaft assembly

Removal:

Remove the engine from the car, remove the cylinder head assembly, cylinder barrel and the pistons, all as described previously. Remove the generator as described in **Chapter 12**.

Unscrew the four bolts shown in **FIG 1:63** retaining the right main bearing holder. Remove the crankcase right side cover. Remove the primary drive assembly and the oil pump as described previously. Unscrew the mounting bolt shown in **FIG 1:64**, noting that an aluminium washer is used.

Invert the engine, but do not support it by the gearshift rod. Separate the lower and upper crankcase halves by removing the 10 6mm (B and C) and eight 8mm bolts (A) shown in **FIG 1:65**, noting those fitted with aluminium washers (C). These washers must be refitted in their original positions, as they prevent oil leakage. Unbolt and remove the crankshaft centre bearing cap, then remove the crankshaft assembly. As the crankshaft assembly is a press-assembled unit, only the right and left main bearing can be renewed separately.

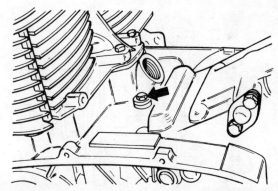

FIG 1:64   The mounting bolt with aluminium washer

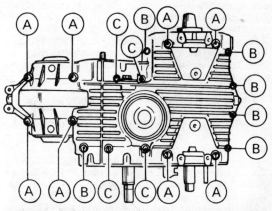

FIG 1:65   The bolts which join the crankcase halves; A = 8mm, B and C = 6mm. C bolts are fitted with aluminium washers

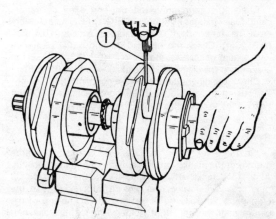

FIG 1:66   Checking big-end axial clearance

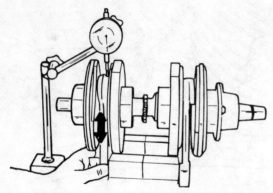

FIG 1:67   Checking big-end radial clearance

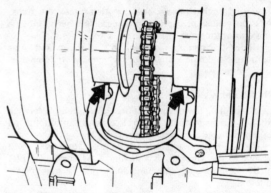

FIG 1:68   Centre bearing oil hole alignment

Servicing:

Mount the crankshaft assembly in a V-block at the centre main bearing position. Rotate the unit slowly while checking with a dial gauge at the right and left main bearing positions, to determine if the shaft is bent. The serviceable limit is 0.04mm (0.0016in). If this is exceeded, correction should be made by tapping the shaft lightly with a soft-faced hammer while supporting at the centre bearing position.

To check the connecting rods for twist or bending, stand the crankshaft assembly horizontally on a surface plate and insert a machined rod 17mm (0.6693in) in diameter and 100mm (3.937in) long through the connecting rod small-end bore. Centralise the rod in the bore.

With the connecting rod held horizontally, measure the distance between each end of the rod and the surface plate. The difference between the two measurements, showing connecting rod twist, must not exceed 0.2mm (0.0079in). With the connecting rod held vertically, measure again in a similar manner. The difference between the two measurements obtained, showing connecting rod bend, must not exceed 0.1mm (0.004in). If any connecting rod is twisted or bent beyond the stated limits, have the fault corrected at a service station if possible, or renew the assembly.

Check the connecting rod big-end axial clearance, using feeler gauges as shown in FIG 1:66. The assembly must be renewed if the clearance exceeds 0.49mm (0.0193in). Check the big-end bearing radial clearance with a dial gauge, as shown in FIG 1:67. Renew the assembly if the clearance exceeds 0.04mm (0.0016in).

Check the inner diameter of the connecting rod small-end, using a dial gauge. If the bore exceeds 17.04mm (0.6709in) in diameter, renew the assembly.

Reassembly:

Fit the cam chain around the crankshaft before mounting the crankshaft in the upper crankcase housing. Align the crankshaft in position with the three dowel pins provided. Two dowel pins fit into recesses in the crankcase parting surface and one fits at the top of the centre main bearing right holder. When the crankshaft and bearings are correctly fitted, the right bearing oil return hole will be pointing towards the top of the engine and the centre bearing oil holes will align with the oil passages as shown in FIG 1:68. This done, fit the centre bearing cap and tighten the bolts evenly to a torque of 3.5 to 4.0kgm (25.31 to 28.93lb ft).

Apply gasket sealing compound to the lower crankcase machined parting surface, install the two dowel pins and assemble the two crankcase halves, fitting the mounting bolts finger tight and correctly installing the aluminium washers. Tighten the bolts alternately and evenly, to a final torque of 0.9 to 1.2 kgm (6.5 to 8.7lb ft) for the 11 6mm bolts, 2.3 to 2.8kgm (16.6 to 20.3lb ft) for the eight 8mm bolts.

Fit the right main bearing holder with the four bolts, tightening to a torque of 0.9 to 1.2kgm (6.5 to 8.7lb ft).

Reassemble the remaining components in the reverse order of removal, referring to the appropriate previous sections.

1:11 Fault diagnosis

(a) Engine will not start

1 Defective coil
2 Faulty capacitor
3 Dirty, pitted or incorrectly set contact points
4 Ignition wires loose or insulation faulty
5 Water on spark plug leads
6 Battery discharged, corrosion of terminals
7 Faulty or jammed starter
8 Vapour lock in fuel pipes
9 Defective fuel pump
10 Overchoking or underchoking
11 Blocked fuel filter or carburetter jet
12 Leaking or sticking valves
13 Valve timing incorrect
14 Ignition timing incorrect

(b) Engine stalls

1 Check 1, 2, 3, 4, 5, 9, 10, 11 and 12 in (a)
2 Sparking plugs defective or gaps incorrect
3 Retarded ignition
4 Mixture too weak
5 Water in fuel system
6 Petrol tank vent blocked
7 Incorrect valve clearances

(c) Engine idles badly

1 Check 2 and 7 in (b)
2 Air leak at manifold joints
3 Carburetter adjustment wrong
4 Air leak in carburetter
5 Over-rich mixture
6 Worn piston rings
7 Worn valve stems or guides
8 Weak exhaust valve springs

(d) Engine misfires

1 Check 2, 3, 4, 5, 9, 11, 12, 13 and 14 in (a)
2 Weak or broken valve springs

(e) Engine overheats (see Chapter 4)

(f) Compression low

1 Check 12 in (a); 6 and 7 in (c) and 2 in (d)
2 Worn piston ring grooves
3 Scored or worn cylinder bores

(g) Engine lacks power

1 Check 3, 9, 10, 11, 12, 13 and 14 in (a); 2, 3, 4 and 7 in (b); 6 and 7 in (c) and 2 in (d). Also check (e) and (f)
2 Leaking joint washers
3 Fouled sparking plugs
4 Automatic advance not working

(h) Burned valves or seats

1 Check 12 and 13 in (a); 7 in (b) and 2 in (d). Also check (e)
2 Excessive carbon around valve seats and heads

(j) Sticking valves

1 Check 2 in (d)
2 Bent valve stem
3 Scored valve stem or guide
4 Incorrect valve clearances

(k) Excessive cylinder wear

1 Lack of oil
2 Dirty oil
3 Piston rings gummed up or broken
4 Badly fitting piston rings
5 Bent connecting rod

(l) Excessive oil consumption

1 Check 6 and 7 in (c) and check (k)
2 Ring gaps too wide
3 Oil return holes in piston choked with carbon
4 Scored cylinders
5 Oil level too high
6 External oil leaks

(m) Crankshaft and connecting rod bearing failure

1 Check 1 in (k)
2 Restricted oilways
3 Worn bearings
4 Loose bearing cap
5 Extremely low oil pressure
6 Bent connecting rod

(n) High fuel consumption (see Chapter 2)

(o) Engine vibration

1 Loose engine mountings
2 Engine mounting rubbers worn or wrongly fitted
3 Exhaust system fitted under stress
4 Misfiring due to mixture, ignition or mechanical faults

NOTES

CHAPTER 2

THE FUEL SYSTEM

2:1 Description

Fuel from the tank passes to the fuel pump and then to the carburetter through a series of rigid and flexible pipes. The fuel pump is electrically operated and incorporates a fuel filter unit.

The Honda CV carburetter has a single large venturi controlled by a throttle valve and vacuum piston and has primary and secondary fuel metering systems incorporated.

The air cleaner is fitted with a paper cartridge filter element and a hot air induction system, which uses a proportion of the engine cooling air to warm the incoming fuel/air mixture.

2:2 Air cleaner

The air cleaner is mounted in the engine compartment on the upper dashboard as shown in **FIG 2:1**. Cold air entering the intake is mixed with hot air from the engine cooling system, the warm air then passing through the filter unit to the carburetter. The engine breather tube is connected to the air cleaner assembly so that crankcase fumes will be harmlessly burned in the combustion chambers. The small accumulation of oil which will result is drained from the air cleaner through a tube. This tube is provided with a slit through which oil is automatically discharged, except on models exported to the USA, where a plug is fitted to prevent any oil loss. On these models, the plug should be removed regularly and the oil drained into a suitable container and discarded.

The air filter element should be removed and cleaned at 3000 mile (5000km) intervals and renewed every 9000 miles (15,000km). These intervals should, however, be reduced as necessary if the vehicle is operated continuously in city traffic or under very dusty conditions.

Filter element servicing:

Remove the wing nut and rubber washers and take off the air cleaner cover. Remove the retainer spring as shown in **FIG 2:2** and lift out the filter element.

Clean the element by blowing compressed air through from the inside. If the element is very dirty or oil contaminated, it should be renewed, even if this is before the recommended mileage has been reached.

Clean accumulated oil and dirt from inside the air cleaner chamber before installing the element. Make sure that the cover is properly sealed and that the rubber washers are installed beneath the retaining wing nuts.

Air cleaner assembly removal:

Remove the air cleaner element as described previously. Remove the bellows retainer and separate it from the

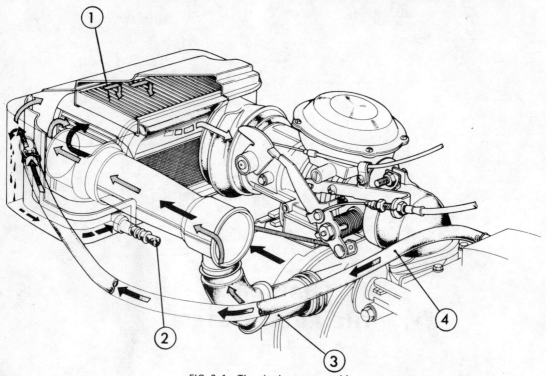

FIG 2:1 The air cleaner assembly

Key to Fig 2:1   1 Air cleaner element   2 Drain plug (USA)   3 Hot air intake   4 Breather tube

carburetter. Remove the two fixing bolts as shown in **FIG 2:3** to release the assembly.

On 600 models from 1969 onwards, the air cleaner mounting has been modified as shown in **FIG 2:4**, using a support and rubber washers.

2:3 Fuel pump

Testing:

Before testing the pump, ensure that the fuel tank vent system is not blocked. If it is suspected that fuel is not reaching the carburetter, disconnect the carburetter feed pipe and hold a suitable container under the end of the pipe. Switch on the ignition for a moment and watch for fuel flow from the pipe, which indicates that the pump is working. If so, check the float needle in the carburetter for possible sticking and the filter screen in the carburetter fuel inlet.

Reduced fuel flow can be caused by blocked fuel pipes or a clogged filter. Check the filter element in the fuel pump. If an obstructed pipeline appears to be the cause of the trouble, it may be cleared with compressed air. Disconnect the pipe at the pump and carburetter. **Do not pass compressed air through the pump or the valves will be damaged.** If there is an obstruction between the pump and the tank, remove the filler cap before blowing the pipe through from the pump end.

If the pump does not operate at all when the ignition is switched on, connect a jumper lead to the positive battery terminal and touch the other end of the lead to the

positive terminal on the pump body. If the pump then operates, the fault lies in the wiring between the battery and ignition switch, or between the switch and the pump.

If the pump does not operate when connected to the battery by jumper lead, check that the pump body is earthing properly against the car frame. Connect a jumper lead between the pump body and a good earth on the car frame to check this point. If the pump then operates, check the pump earth cable and its contact at the mounting bolt, clean the connection and retighten.

If the pump fails to operate after all tests, it must be renewed, as no repairs are possible on the electromagnetic components.

Removal:

Disconnect the leads at the connector and remove the fuel pipes from the inlet of the fuel strainer and the outlet of the fuel pump, as shown in **FIG 2:5**. Remove the mounting bolts from the fuel pump and remove the unit from the car. Do not attempt to dismantle the pump unit.

Refitting is a reversal of the removal procedure.

Fuel filter element renewal:

Remove the pump and strainer assembly as just described, then remove and discard the complete strainer unit (see **FIG 2:6**), which is of the sealed cartridge type. Fit a new strainer unit and refit in the reverse order of removal.

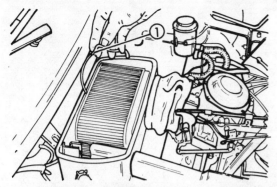

FIG 2:2   Air filter element removal

Key to Fig 2:2   1 Retainer spring

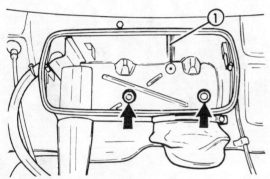

FIG 2:3   Air cleaner assembly removal

Key to Fig 2:3   1 Groove retainer for spring

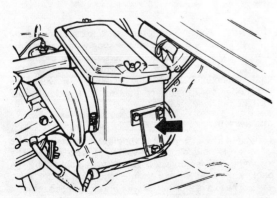

FIG 2:4   Modified air cleaner mounting, 600 models from 1969

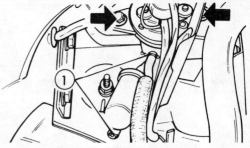

FIG 2:5   Fuel pump removal

Key to Fig 2:5   1 Fuel pipes

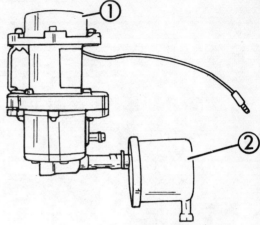

FIG 2:6   Fuel strainer removal

Key to Fig 2:6   1 Fuel pump   2 Fuel strainer

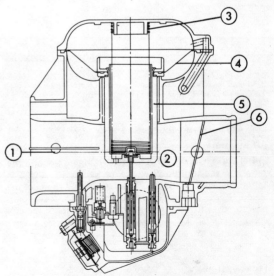

FIG 2:7   Carburetter air system

Key to Fig 2:7   1 Air intake   2 Venturi   3 Vacuum piston spring   4 Diaphragm   5 Vacuum piston   6 Throttle valve

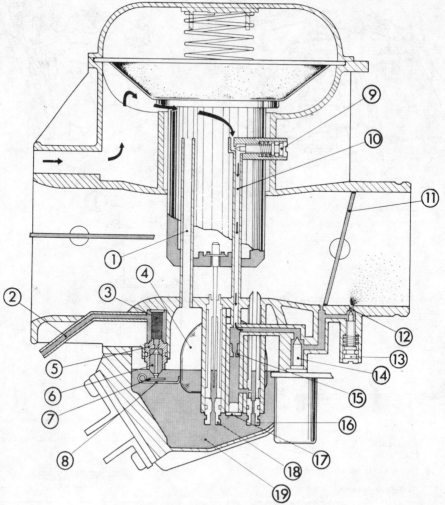

FIG 2:8 Carburetter float and idle systems

Key to Fig 2:8   1 Air vent   2 Fuel duct   3 Filter   4 Float   5 Needle valve body   6 Needle valve   7 Tag   8 Float arm
9 Idle air jet screw   10 Idle air duct   11 Throttle valve   12 Idle orifice   13 Idle volume control screw   14 Fuel solenoid valve
15 Idle jet   16 Primary main jet   17 Plug   18 Secondary main jet   19 Float chamber

2:4 Carburetter operation

Air system:

Refer to **FIG 2:7**. Air is fed to the engine through the venturi 2 and throttle valve 6. The vacuum piston 5 is spring-loaded towards the closed position. When engine speed is low, at small throttle openings, the vacuum piston moves to its lowest position, becoming a primary venturi maintaining a constant airflow. As the airflow and vacuum increase, the piston rises to maintain the required air volume.

Float system:

Refer to **FIG 2:8**. Fuel enters the carburetter through the fuel strainer 3 and passes through the needle valve assembly 5 and 6 into the float chamber 19. As the level of fuel in the chamber rises, the float 4 presses upwards on the needle valve 6 to cut off the supply and maintain a constant fuel level. As fuel is used, the float drops and allows more fuel to enter through the needle valve. The float movement is damped by a spring, to prevent road vibrations from causing the float to move suddenly and damage the needle valve.

Idle system:

Refer to **FIG 2:8**. When the engine is idling, the throttle valve 11 is held almost closed by a stop screw. The incoming fuel is subjected to coarse regulation by the primary main jet 16 and to fine regulation by the slow jet 15. The fuel is then mixed with the air supplied through the idle air passage 10 before being ejected through the pilot outlet 12 connected to the solenoid valve 14. Fine

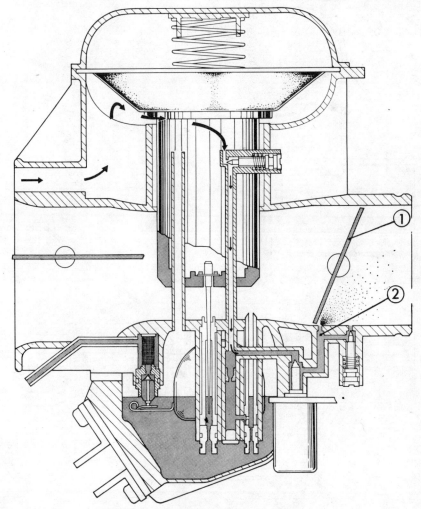

FIG 2:9 Carburetter off-idle system

Key to Fig 2:9   1 Throttle valve   2 Orifice discharge port

adjustment of the idle mixture is obtained by turning the pilot screw 13, fine adjustment of the idle speed by turning the throttle stop screw.

The slow air jet 9 is fixed on 360 models but adjustable on 600 models, although adjustment should not be required as the setting is factory made. The correct adjustment of the screw on 600 models is 1½ turns out from the fully closed position, corresponding to an orifice diameter of 1.2mm (0.047in).

Off-idle system:

Refer to **FIG 2:9**. As the throttle 1 is opened slightly, extra fuel is admitted through the orifice discharge port 2 to mix with the additional air entering through the throttle valve. The supply of fuel is regulated by the amount of air passing through the primary main air jet.

Medium speed system:

Refer to **FIG 2:10**. In the medium speed range the throttle valve 4 will be opened further than in the off-idle state, but not yet to the point where the vacuum piston 5 starts to move. Under these conditions, fuel is supplied through the primary main jet 7, mixed with air from the primary main air jet 3 and ejected through the primary main jet nozzle 6.

High speed system:

Refer to **FIG 2:11**. As the throttle is opened beyond the medium speed position, the vacuum piston 3 starts to move upwards and increase the size of the main venturi progressively, acting against its return spring 1 and the needle 4 is raised in the secondary main jet 8. Fuel then

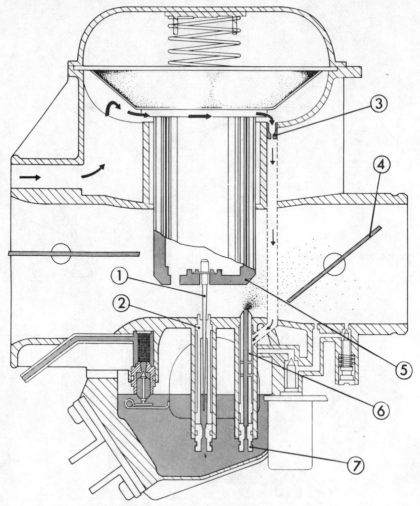

FIG 2:10 Carburetter medium speed system

Key to Fig 2:10 1 Jet needle 2 Secondary main jet nozzle 3 Primary main air jet 4 Throttle valve 5 Vacuum piston 6 Primary main jet nozzle 7 Primary main jet

enters through this jet to supplement that supplied through the primary main jet, being mixed with and regulated by air passing through the secondary main air jet 7. The wider the throttle opening the higher the piston will move, thus increasing the volume of fuel supplied through the secondary jet system in accordance with the volume of air flowing through the main venturi.

Acceleration system:

Refer to **FIG 2:12**. When the throttle is opened suddenly for acceleration, extra fuel is needed to maintain a proper mixture as the volume of incoming air increases rapidly. When the accelerator is depressed, the accelerator pump rod 5 is operated by a linkage. The pump rod 5 presses against a diaphragm 3, which forces fuel from the pump chamber 6 through the pump discharge nozzle 1 to mix with the main air stream. As the accelerator is released, the diaphragm returns to the rest position 8 under spring action and the pump chamber refills with fuel. Fuel flow through the pump is controlled by inlet 7 and outlet 2 check valves.

Starting system:

Refer to **FIG 2:13**. To ensure provision of the extra-rich mixture needed for cold starting, a choke unit and fast-idle linkage are provided. When the choke control is actuated from inside the car, the throttle lever 3 is operated through the choke link cam 1 to provide a higher idling speed by opening the throttle a pre-determined amount. The choke valve closes at the same time, causing a higher than normal vacuum in the main venturi, causing the fuel jets to supply a greater quantity of fuel. As the throttle is opened under these conditions, the choke valve will open according to main venturi

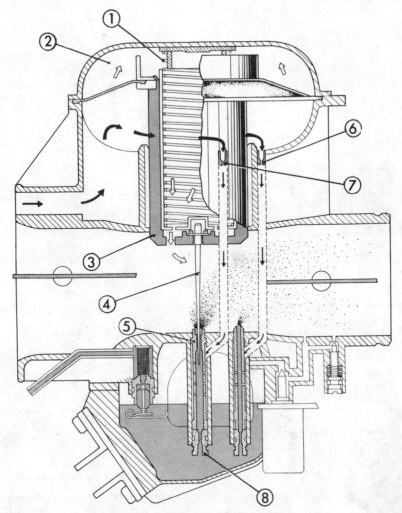

FIG 2:11 Carburetter high speed system

Key to Fig 2:11   1 Vacuum piston spring   2 Vacuum chamber   3 Vacuum piston   4 Jet needle   5 Secondary main jet nozzle   6 Primary main air jet   7 Secondary main air jet   8 Secondary main jet

vacuum, to ensure a regulated rich mixture. When the choke control is returned to the off position, the carburetter is reset in the normal idle position.

2:5 Carburetter adjustments

The idle speed adjustments described in this section should be carried out whenever any carburetter, ignition system or valve clearance adjustments or servicing have been made, or at any time if engine idling is rough or at too high a speed.

If poor performance is traced to the carburetter, the remaining adjustments given should be carried out. If the faults are not cured by these adjustments, the carburetter should be removed and serviced as described later and, on completion, the adjustments carried out again. Always make the idle speed adjustment last.

It must be stressed that carburetter adjustments will only be effective if the sparking plugs, ignition system and valve clearances are in order. The engine must be at normal operating temperature, with the air cleaner fitted, when idle speed adjustments are made.

Idle speed adjustment:

Refer to **FIG 2:14**. If the pilot screw 2 has been disturbed, set it to a basic position by tightening it lightly onto its seat and unscrewing it $\frac{5}{8}$ of a turn on 360 models, $1\frac{1}{2}$ to 2 turns on 600 models. Start the engine and adjust the throttle stop screw 1 to obtain an engine speed of approximately 1100rev/min. In the absence of a tachometer, set the speed so that the charge indicator lamp on the instrument panel goes out when the accelerator pedal is slightly depressed.

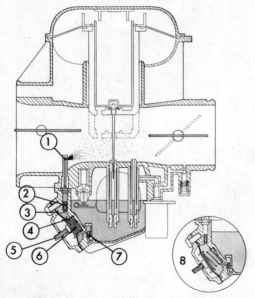

FIG 2:12 Carburetter acceleration system

Key to Fig 2:12   1 Discharge nozzle   2 Check valve
3 Diaphragm   4 Diaphragm spring   5 Pump rod   6 Pump
chamber   7 Check valve   8 Suction stroke

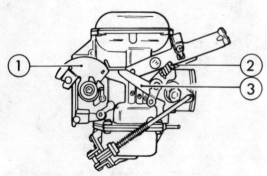

FIG 2:13 Carburetter starting system

Key to Fig 2:13   1 Choke cam   2 Throttle stop   3 Lever

FIG 2:14 Carburetter throttle stop 1 and pilot screw 2

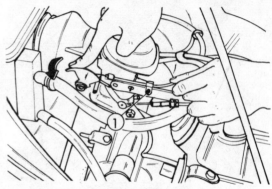

FIG 2:15 Choke cable adjustment

Key to Fig 2:15   1 Adjusting screw

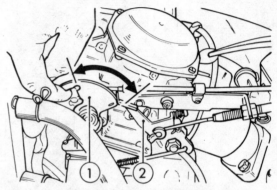

FIG 2:16 Fast-idle adjustment

Key to Fig 2:16   1 Fast-idle cam   2 Throttle lever

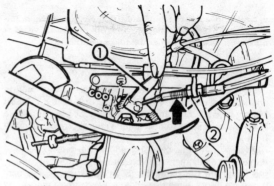

FIG 2:17 Throttle adjustment

Key to Fig 2:17   1 Throttle lever   2 Cable adjusting nuts

Now turn the pilot screw, a little at a time, in or out as necessary, to obtain the highest possible idling speed without touching the throttle stop screw. This done, lower the speed to the correct setting by turning the throttle stop screw. If necessary, make a further slight adjustment to the pilot screw to smooth the idle. Accelerate the engine, allow it to settle back at idle and recheck the speed. If the idle speed has changed, check the throttle linkage for binding before resetting the idle speed.

Choke adjustment:

Refer to **FIG 2:15** and adjust the choke cable so that the choke is fully open when the choke button is in the off position.

Fast-idle adjustment:

When the choke valve is operated, the fast-idle cam opens the throttle valve slightly by contacting the throttle lever. To adjust, refer to **FIG 2:16** and loosen the throttle valve stop screw to allow the valve to close fully. Then, bend the throttle lever 2 so that the fast-idle cam 1 starts to lift the throttle lever at the punch mark.

Throttle adjustment:

Refer to **FIG 2:17**. Have an assistant fully depress the accelerator pedal, then check that the throttle valve is fully open 1. If not, adjust by means of the cable adjusting nuts 2.

Fuel solenoid valve:

The fuel solenoid valve, shown in **FIG 2:18**, is mounted on the carburetter and operates electrically to open the idle fuel passage when the ignition is switched on. This prevents fuel loss when the engine is stopped. No adjustments are possible but, if the engine cannot be made to idle correctly, the valve should be checked in the following manner:

With the car parked in a quiet area, open the bonnet and switch on the ignition. Disconnect and reconnect the solenoid lead at its connector while checking for an operating sound or vibration, which will indicate that the solenoid is operating. If not, make the test with a jumper lead from the battery. If the solenoid then operates, the fault is in the wiring or ignition switch; if not, the solenoid is defective and must be renewed.

A temporary measure can be taken to allow the car to run until the unit can be renewed by removing the solenoid and blanking off the port with a flat plate, or by fixing the valve with the plunger depressed by suitable means. This does mean, however, that flooding may occur when the engine is switched off.

Accelerator pump:

Measure the accelerator pump stroke at the point shown in **FIG 2:19**. Find the setting mark which is stamped on the outside of the carburetter body, then refer to **Technical Data** to find the correct pump stroke. To adjust, move the cotterpin 1 to a different hole or turn the adjusting nuts, according to the type of pump rod fitted.

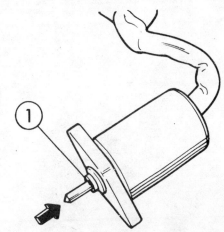

FIG 2:18 The fuel solenoid valve

Key to Fig 2:18   1 Valve

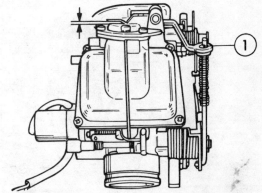

FIG 2:19 Typical accelerator pump stroke measurement and adjustment point 1

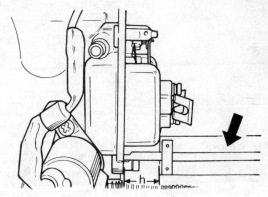

FIG 2:20 Float level adjustment

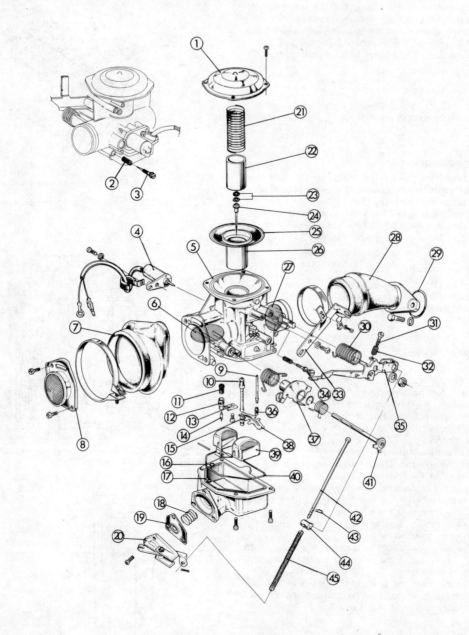

FIG 2:21 Carburetter components

Key to Fig 2:21   1 Cap   2 Spring   3 Volume control screw   4 Fuel solenoid valve   5 Carburetter body   6 Choke valve   7 Bellows   8 Screen   9 Primary main jet nozzle   10 Secondary main jet nozzle   11 Filter   12 Needle valve body   13 Retainer   14 Needle valve   15 Secondary main jet   16 'O' ring   17 Float chamber   18 Spring   19 Diaphragm   20 Accelerator pump lever assembly   21 Vacuum piston spring   22 Jet needle retainer   23 Shims   24 Jet needle   25 Diaphragm   26 Vacuum piston   27 Throttle valve   28 Intake manifold   29 'O' ring   30 Return spring   31 Throttle stop screw   32 Spring   33 Cable stay adaptor   34 Idle air jet screw   35 Throttle lever   36 Primary main jet   37 Choke link cam   38 Main jet retainer   39 Float   40 'O' ring   41 Choke valve spindle   42 Accelerator pump rod   43 Spring clip   44 Pump rod retainer   45 Spring

Float level:

Remove the carburetter body and hold the assembly as shown in **FIG 2:20**. Move the float gently back and forth and locate the point where the tip of the float arm barely touches the tip of the needle valve. In this position, measure dimension **h** and compare with the figures given in **Technical Data**. Adjust by carefully bending the float arm.

2:6 Carburetter servicing

Removal:

Disconnect the fuel line and the throttle and choke linkages, then remove the carburetter from the vehicle.

Dismantling:

Dismantle the carburetter into the order shown in **FIG 2:21**, carefully noting the positions of the components and laying them out on a clean sheet of paper. Mark shafts and levers so that they will be reassembled in their correct relative positions. Avoid dismantling the throttle and choke valves as they are accurately factory-assembled.

The primary 2 and secondary 1 main air jets are force-fitted as shown in **FIG 2:22** and cannot be removed, but the slow air jet 4 is attached by screws. The accelerator pump check valve collar is made of resin and should not be dismantled.

Cleaning and inspection:

Clean all parts in petrol or an approved carburetter cleaner, then inspect them for wear or damage. Renew any faulty parts. Clean jets and passages thoroughly, using compressed air, clean petrol and a small, nylon brush. **Do not use cloth for cleaning purposes, as small fibres may remain after cleaning and clog the jets. Never use a wire probe as this will damage or enlarge the jets.** If a jet has a blockage that cannot be cleared with compressed air, use a single bristle from a nylon brush for the purpose. If this method is unsuccessful, renew the jet.

Make sure that all sediment is cleared from the float chamber 17 (see **FIG 2:21**) and inspect the floats 39 for damage or leakage, either of which will dictate renewal of the float assembly. Float leakage can usually be detected by shaking the float and listening for fuel splash inside.

Check the float needle valve assembly 12 and 14 carefully, renewing the assembly if there is any sign of a ridge on the tapered valve seat 14. A damaged needle valve can lead to flooding by failing to cut off the fuel supply properly when the float chamber is full, or may stick in the closed position and prevent sufficient fuel from reaching the float chamber.

Examine the carburetter fuel filter 11 and renew it if it is deformed or damaged, or if it will not clean up properly. Inspect the main jet 'O' rings 1, as shown in **FIG 2:23**, for damage or stretching and renew them if necessary. Clean the interior of the accelerator pump and inspect the diaphragm, spring and check valve.

Assembling:

This is a reversal of the dismantling procedure, noting the following points.

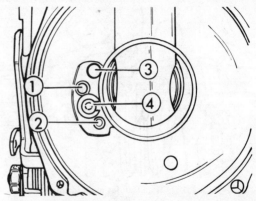

FIG 2:22   The air jets and vent

Key to Fig 2:22   1 Secondary air jet   2 Primary air jet   3 Air vent   4 Slow air jet

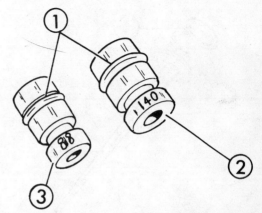

FIG 2:23   The main jet 'O' rings 1, secondary main jet 2 and primary main jet 3

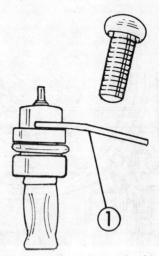

FIG 2:24   Valve seat retainer spring 1 installation

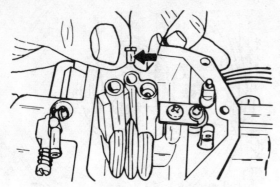

FIG 2:25　The slow jet sealing plug

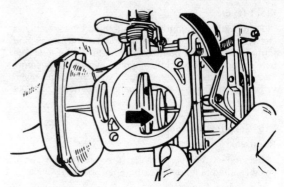

FIG 2:28　Checking vacuum piston movement

Note the correct direction of the bend in the valve seat retainer spring shown in **FIG 2:24** and ensure that it is not installed in reverse. Adjust the float level as described in **Section 2:5**.

Make sure that the slow jet sealing plug is securely installed, as shown in **FIG 2:25**. Ensure that the 'O' ring is installed in the accelerator pump passage outlet. Two adjusting shims 1 are provided at the top and bottom of the jet needle 2 at the upper flange, as shown in **FIG 2:26**. In very cold climates, two shims can be fitted in the lower position to richen the mixture.

After installing the jet needle on the vacuum piston, install the jet needle retainer into the piston and attach with the vacuum piston spring. There is a small protruding section on the vacuum piston upper diaphragm, which must be aligned with the groove on the carburetter body, as shown in **FIG 2:27**. Check the action of the vacuum piston by installing the carburetter cover without the spring and and tilting the unit as shown in **FIG 2:28**. If the piston slides under its own weight, the operation is satisfactory.

Carry out the adjustments given in **Section 2:5** when the carburetter has been fully assembled, the idle speed adjustments being made after installation and warm-up.

Refit the carburetter to the car in the reverse order of removal.

2:7 Fault diagnosis

(a) Leakage or insufficient fuel delivered

1 Air vent to tank restricted
2 Fuel pipes blocked
3 Air leaks at pipe connections
4 Fuel filter blocked
5 Fuel pump internally defective
6 Fuel pump wiring faulty

(b) Excessive fuel consumption

1 Carburetter requires adjustment
2 Fuel leakage
3 Sticking choke control
4 Float level too high
5 Dirty air cleaner
6 Worn carburetter jets
7 Excessive engine temperature
8 Idling speed too high

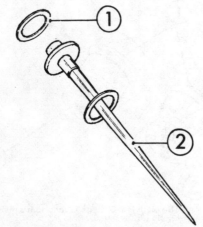

FIG 2:26　The jet needle 2 and shims 1

FIG 2:27　Aligning the vacuum piston diaphragm

(c) Idling speed too high

1 Rich fuel mixture
2 Carburetter incorrectly adjusted
3 Throttle control sticking
4 Choke control sticking
5 Worn throttle valve

(d) Noisy fuel pump

1 Loose pump mountings
2 Air leaks on suction side of pump

3 Obstruction in pipeline
4 Clogged fuel filter

(e) No fuel delivery

1 Float needle valve stuck
2 Tank vent system blocked
3 Defective fuel pump
4 Pump wiring faulty
5 Pipeline obstructed
6 Bad air leak on suction side of pump

NOTES

CHAPTER 3

THE IGNITION SYSTEM

3 : 1 Description

The ignition system consists of the battery, ignition coil, contact breaker assembly, sparking plugs and HT and LT wiring. As the two engine cylinders fire simultaneously, no conventional distributor is needed. The contact breaker assembly incorporates automatic timing control by centrifugal mechanism and a vacuum operated unit.

As engine speed increases, the centrifugal action of rotating weights pivoting against the tension of small springs moves the contact breaker assembly relative to its drive shaft and progressively advances the ignition. The vacuum control unit is connected by small bore pipe to the engine intake system. At high degrees of engine inlet vacuum the unit advances the ignition, but under load, at reduced vacuum, the unit progressively retards the ignition.

The ignition coil is wound as an auto-transformer, with the primary and secondary windings connected in series, the common junction being connected to the contact breaker with the positive feed from the battery going to the opposite terminal of the LT winding, via the ignition switch.

When the contacts are closed, current flows in the coil primary winding, magnetising the core and setting up a fairly strong magnetic field. Each time the contacts open, the battery current is cut off and the magnet field collapses, inducing a high current in the primary winding and a high voltage in the secondary. The primary current is used to charge the capacitor connected across the contacts and the flow is high and virtually instantaneous. It is this high current peak which induces the surge in the secondary winding to produce the sparking voltage across the plug points. Without the capacitor, the current would be much smaller and the sparking voltage considerably reduced, in fact to a point where it would be insufficient to fire the mixture in the engine cylinders. The capacitor, therefore, serves the dual purpose of minimising contact breaker point wear and providing the necessary high charging surge to ensure a powerful spark.

3 : 2 Routine maintenance

About every 5000km (3000 miles) remove the contact breaker cover and apply a small drop of oil to the pivot point of the moving contact breaker. Wipe clean the cam which opens the points, then apply a thin smear of grease to the cam. When lubricating the internal parts of the contact breaker assembly, take great care to avoid oil or grease contaminating the contact breaker points, lubricating sparingly for this reason.

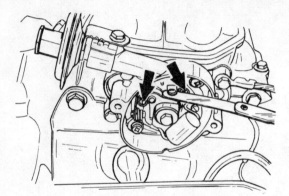

FIG 3:1   Checking the contact points gap

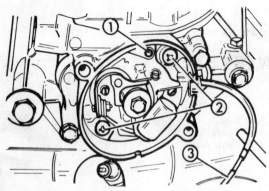

FIG 3:2   Contact breaker assembly removal

Key to Fig 3:2   1 Snap ring   2 Screws   3 Primary lead

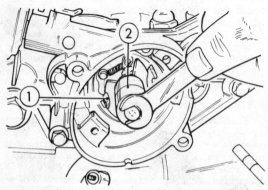

FIG 3:3   Removing the cam 2 and centrifugal advance unit 1

Adjusting the contact breaker points:

Remove the contact breaker cover as shown in **FIG 3:1**. Turn the engine until the cam has opened the contact points to their fullest extent, then check the gap between the points with clean feeler gauges. The correct gap is 0.3 to 0.4mm (0.012 to 0.016in). To adjust the gap, loosen the adjusting screws and move the fixed contact point. Tighten the screws and recheck the gap.

Cleaning the contact points:

Use a fine carborundum stone or a special contact file to polish the points if they are dirty or pitted, taking care to keep the faces flat and square. If the points are too worn to clean up in this manner, they should be renewed. The contact points can be removed for replacement or for cleaning, if required, as described later. After cleaning, wipe away all dust with a cloth moistened in petrol.

3:3 Ignition faults

If the engine runs unevenly or misfires, set it to idle at about 1000rev/min and, taking care not to touch any conducting part of the sparking plug leads, remove and replace each lead from its plug in turn. To avoid shocks during this operation, it is best to wear a pair of thick gloves or to use insulated pliers. Doing this to a plug which is firing properly will accentuate the uneven running or cause the engine to stop running altogether, but will make little or no difference if the plug is not firing correctly.

Having by this means located the faulty cylinder, stop the engine and remove the plug lead. Remove the plug connector so that the lead is exposed. Start the engine and hold the lead about $\frac{1}{8}$in away from the cylinder head. A strong, regular spark confirms that the fault lies with the sparking plug which should be removed and cleaned as described in **Section 3:6**, or renewed if defective.

If the spark is weak or irregular, check the condition of the lead and, if it is worn or perished, renew it and repeat the test. If no improvement results, check that there is no internal shortcircuit in the contact breaker unit and that the LT circuit is in order.

Testing the LT circuit:

Check that the contact breaker points are clean and correctly set, then proceed as follows:

Disconnect the thin wire from the coil that connects to the contact breaker unit. Remove the sparking plugs to make the engine easier to turn and to prevent the engine from firing. Disconnect the thin wire that connects between the coil and the contact breaker unit. Switch on the ignition and turn the engine slowly. An easy way to do this is to select top gear, release the handbrake and push the car backwards or forwards as necessary. Make sure that the car is on level ground during the operation. If, when the contact points close, the lamp lights and, when they open, goes out, the circuit is in order. If the lamp fails to light, there is a fault in the LT circuit.

If the fault lies in the LT circuit, use the test lamp to carry out the following tests, with the ignition switched on.

Disconnect the wire from the ignition switch side of the coil and connect the lamp between the end of this wire and earth. If the lamp fails to light it indicates a fault in the wiring or connections between the battery and the coil, or in the ignition switch. Reconnect the wire if the lamp lights.

Disconnect the wire from the coil that leads to the contact breaker. Connect the lamp between the coil terminal and earth. If the lamp fails to light it indicates a fault in the primary winding and a new coil must be fitted.

Reconnect the wire if the lamp lights and disconnect its other end from the contact breaker assembly. If the lamp does not light when connected between the end of the wire and earth, it indicates a fault in that section of wire.

Capacitor:

The best method of testing a capacitor is by substitution. Disconnect the original capacitor and connect a new one between the LT terminal on the contact breaker assembly and earth, for test purposes. If a new capacitor is proved to be required, it can then be properly fitted. The capacitor is of 0.22 microfarad capacity.

3:4 Removing and dismantling contact breaker

Remove the contact breaker cover and pull off the snap ring 1 which retains the vacuum unit rod to the breaker plate, then disconnect the primary lead 3 at the connector. Remove the breaker plate set screws 2, shown in **FIG 3:2**, and remove the breaker assembly.

Remove the bolt shown in **FIG 3:3** and pull out the breaker cam 2 and spark advance mechanism 1. Refer to **FIG 3:4** and check the advance springs 3 for damage, distortion or loss of tension and the weight pin 2 for excessive wear. Renew any faulty parts and lightly lubricate the moving parts of the assembly.

Check the right camshaft holder for oil leaks. If leaks are found, check the oil seal for defects and check the camshaft for excessive axial play. A faulty check valve on the camshaft chain tensioner can also be responsible for oil leaks.

Refitting:

Refitting is a reversal of the removal procedure, noting the following points:

When refitting the spark advance mechanism, align the groove 3 or the advance mechanism and the dowel pin 2 on the camshaft, as shown in **FIG 3:5**. Check the condition of the contact points as described previously, cleaning or renewing them as necessary.

When refitting the breaker assembly or capacitor, make sure that the insulating washers 1 are fitted in the correct order, as shown in **FIG 3:6**. If they are fitted incorrectly, the assembly will be shortcircuited and the engine will not run. Check the ignition timing.

3:5 Timing the ignition

Remove the contact breaker cover and turn the engine until the pistons are at the top of their travel on the compression stroke. To do this, remove a sparking plug and turn the engine until compression can be felt by a thumb placed over the spark plug hole. Now turn the engine a little more as necessary until the timing mark F

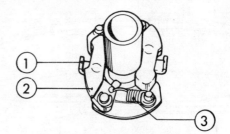

FIG 3:4   The centrifugal advance mechanism

Key to Fig 3:4   1 Weight stop   2 Weights   3 Spring

on the crankshaft pulley is aligned with the mark on the generator cover, as shown in **FIG 3:7**.

Connect a 12-volt test lamp in parallel with the contact breaker points. One lead will go to the terminal on the contact breaker assembly and one to earth. Switch on the ignition. Adjust the timing as shown in **FIG 3:8** by moving the vacuum unit 1 in or out. The vacuum unit should be moved slowly until the light just goes out, which indicates that the contact points are just opening to fire the cylinder. Secure the vacuum unit and recheck the setting.

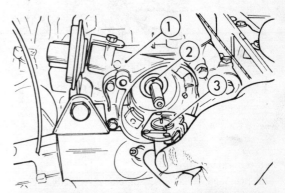

FIG 3:5   Aligning the advance mechanism and the camshaft dowel pin 2, the camshaft holder 1 and the groove 3

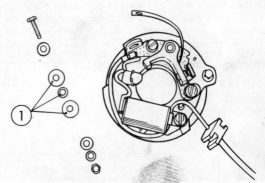

FIG 3:6   Fitting the insulating washers 1

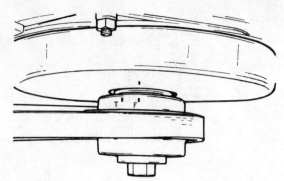

FIG 3:7 Aligning the ignition timing marks

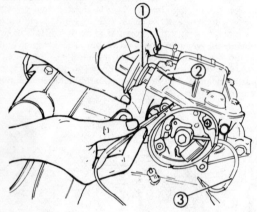

FIG 3:8 Setting the ignition timing

Key to Fig 3:8 1 Vacuum unit 2 Bolt 3 Primary lead

3:6 Sparking plugs

Inspect and clean sparking plugs regularly. When removing sparking plugs, ensure that their recesses are clean and dry so that nothing can fall into the cylinders. Plug gaskets can be re-used, provided that they are not less than half their original thickness. Have sparking plugs cleaned on an abrasive-blasting machine and tested under pressure with the electrode gaps correctly set at 0.7 to 0.8mm (0.028 to 0.032in). Alternatively, clean the electrodes with a steel wire brush. The electrodes should be filed until they are bright and parallel. The gaps must always be set by bending the earth electrode. **Never attempt to bend the centre electrode.**

Before refitting the plugs, clean the threads with a wire brush. Clean the threads in the cylinder head if the plugs cannot be screwed in by hand. Failing a tap for this purpose, use an old spark plug with crosscuts down the threads. Plugs should be tightened with a proper plug spanner, through half-a-turn extra over finger tightness. Other types of spanner may slip off during tightening and crack the plug insulation.

Inspection of the deposits on the electrodes can be helpful when tuning. Normally, from mixed periods of high and low speed driving, the deposits will be powdery and range in colour from brown to greyish-tan. There will also be slight wear of the electrodes. Long periods of constant speed driving or low speed city driving will give white or yellowish deposits. Dry, black fluffy deposits are due to incomplete combustion and indicate running with a rich mixture, excessive idling and, possibly, defective ignition. Overheated plugs have a white blistered look about the centre electrode and the side electrode may be badly eroded. This may be caused by poor cooling, incorrect ignition or sustained high speeds with heavy loads.

Black, wet deposits result from oil in the combustion chamber from worn pistons, rings, valve stems or guides. Sparking plugs which run hotter may alleviate the problem, but the cure is an engine overhaul.

3:7 Fault diagnosis

(a) Engine will not fire

1 Battery discharged
2 Contact points dirty, pitted or maladjusted
3 Oil or dirt on contact breaker points
4 Faulty cable or loose connection in LT circuit
5 Faulty coil
6 Broken contact breaker spring
7 Contact points stuck open

(b) Engine misfires

1 Check 2, 3 and 5 in (a)
2 Weak contact breaker spring
3 HT plug or coil lead cracked or perished
4 Sparking plug(s) loose
5 Sparking plug insulation cracked
6 Sparking plug gaps incorrectly set
7 Ignition timing too far advanced

(c) Poor acceleration

1 Ignition retarded
2 Centrifugal weights seized
3 Centrifugal springs weak, broken or disconnected
4 Excessive contact points gap
5 Worn plugs
6 Faulty vacuum unit or leaking line

CHAPTER 4

THE COOLING SYSTEM

4:1 Description

The air-cooling system consists of a fan driven by a belt from the crankshaft pulley, shrouds and ducting which direct the air over the finned engine cylinder units. The layout of the system is shown in **FIG 4:1**. The fan 2 is encased in the heater drum 1, hot air being directed to the car interior when the heater control is operated.

Maintenance is restricted to an occasional check on the condition and tension of the fan drive belt. The cylinder fins should be kept clear of dirt to ensure a clear passage for the cooling air and to avoid objectionable fumes from entering the passengers compartment through the heating system.

4:2 Fan belt tensioning

Check the belt tension by narrowing it with the fingers as shown in **FIG 4:2**, at a point midway between the pulleys. The distance between the inside edges of the belt should then be 20mm (0.80in).

To adjust the belt, loosen the adjusting nut on the idler pulley and move the pulley until the tension is correct. Tighten the adjusting nut and recheck the tension.

Removing the belt:

Loosen the adjusting nut 2 and push the idler pulley 1 as far as possible towards the engine, as shown in **FIG**

4:3. Remove the belt from the idler pulley, crankshaft pulley and fan pulley. Pull out the belt as shown in **FIG 4:4**, with the idler pulley 1 moved to the outside. Refitting is a reversal of the removal procedure.

4:3 Cooling air shrouds

Removal:

The cooling air shrouds 1 (see **FIG 4:5**) are installed on both sides of the camshaft housing, each shroud being secured in three places by rubber-insulated mountings 3.

Remove the two upper mounting bolts 2 and pull the shroud 1 upwards. Refit in the reverse order of removal, making sure that the cylinder cooling fins are clean.

4:4 Cooling fan

Removal:

Remove the fan belt as described previously. Unscrew the four mounting bolts and remove the fan housing from the engine. The heater drum is installed with two bolts through leaf springs.

Check the cooling fan bearing for roughness or wear. If renewal is necessary, pull the fan pulley 5 out and remove the bearings 2 and 4 as shown in **FIG 4:6**. A conventional puller tool should be used for this operation.

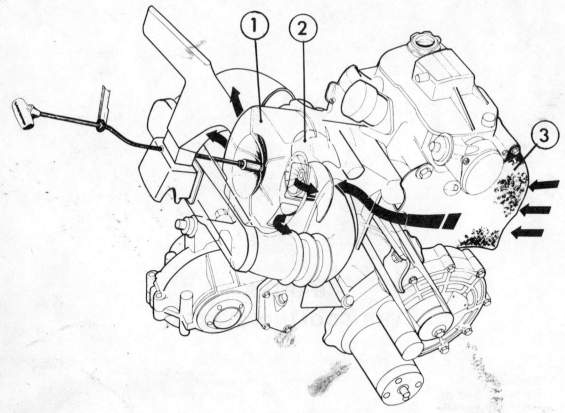

FIG 4:1   Layout of the cooling system

Key to Fig 4:1   1 Heater drum   2 Cooling fan   3 Cooling air shroud

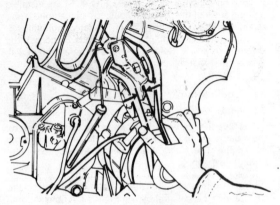

FIG 4:2   Fan belt tensioning

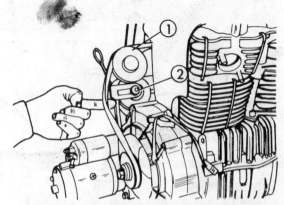

FIG 4:3   The idler pulley 1 and adjusting nut 2

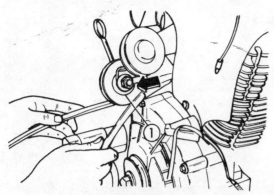

FIG 4:4   Removing the fan belt

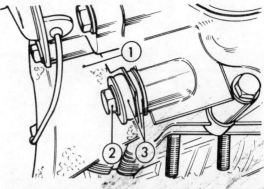

FIG 4:5   Cooling shroud mountings

If new bearings are fitted, a new pulley should also be installed. Make sure that the new pulley is pressed squarely onto the shaft. Check the idler pulley bearings for wear and also check the condition of the heater stop spring. Renew any defective parts.

Refitting:

This is a reversal of the removal operation, checking the belt tension as described in **Section 4:2** on completion.

4:5 Fault diagnosis

(a) Overheating

1 Loose or broken drive belt
2 Loose or missing shroud
3 Cylinder fins choked with dirt
4 Shrouds or ducting blocked

(b) Poor heater performance

1 Loose or missing shroud
2 Blocked heater ducting
3 Faulty heater control

(c) Heater odours

1 Dirt, oil or grease on engine
2 Faulty engine gaskets or seals

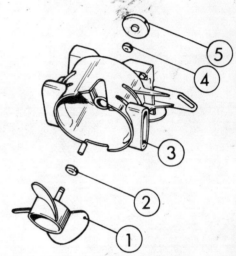

FIG 4:6   The fan and bearing assembly

Key to Fig 4:6   1 Cooling fan   2 Bearing   3 Housing
4 Bearing   5 Pulley

NOTES

CHAPTER 5

THE CLUTCH

5:1 Description

The clutch is a single dry plate unit of diaphragm spring type. Power is transmitted from the engine crankshaft to the clutch by means of the primary drive chains, then transmitted from the clutch unit to the gearbox and transmission.

The driven plate consists of a resilient steel disc attached to a hub which slides on the splined clutch shaft. The friction linings are riveted to both sides of the disc.

The pressure plate assembly consists of the pressure plate, diaphragm spring and housing, the assembly being bolted to the clutch drum. The release bearing is a ball-bearing of special construction with an elongated outer ring that presses directly against the diaphragm spring when the pedal is operated. The bearing is mounted on a carrier and operated from a fork and pivot rod journalled in the clutch housing.

The clutch pedal movement is transmitted to the release bearing by a sheathed steel cable attached to the release lever.

When the clutch is fully engaged, the driven plate is nipped between the pressure plate and the clutch drum and transmits torque to the gearbox through the splined shaft. When the clutch pedal is depressed, the pressure plate is withdrawn from the driven plate by force transmitted through the cable and the driven plate ceases to transmit torque to the gearbox.

5:2 Adjusting the clutch

Clutch adjustment should be checked regularly, as normal wear of the driven plate linings will alter the adjustment in service. If the cable is adjusted with insufficient free play, the cable will be tight and tend to prevent the clutch from engaging properly, causing slip and rapid clutch wear. If the cable has too much free play, the clutch will not release properly, causing drag and consequent poor gearchange qualitites and difficulty in engaging gears from rest.

Adjustments should be carried out in the order given, first at the pedal and lastly at the release lever.

Pedal height adjustment:

The clutch pedal height should be set so that the pedal pad is level with the pad on the brake pedal. To do this, loosen the locknut 2 and tighten or loosen the adjusting bolt 1, then tighten the locknut (see **FIG 5:1**).

FIG 5:1   Clutch pedal height adjustment

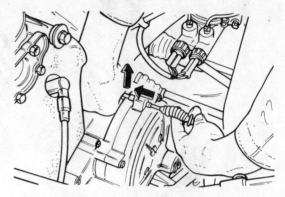

FIG 5:4   Removing the cable from the clutch cover

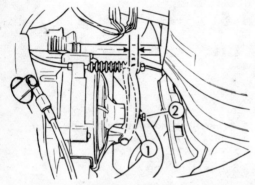

FIG 5:2   Clutch pedal free play adjustment

Key to Fig 5:2   1 Adjusting bolt   2 Locknut

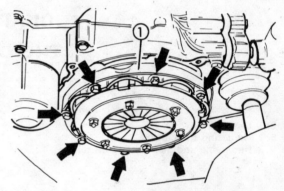

FIG 5:5 Removing the clutch pressure plate assembly 1

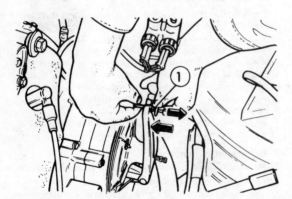

FIG 5:3   Separating the cable from the release lever

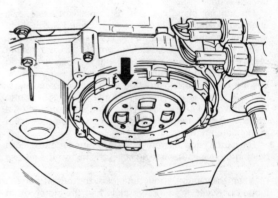

FIG 5:6   Removing the friction plate

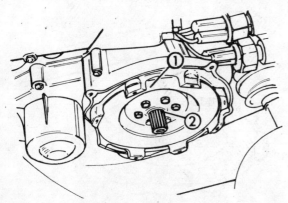

FIG 5:7 Removing the clutch drum 1

FIG 5:8 Pressure plate dismantling

Clutch pedal free play:

This is adjusted to give 3mm (0.12in) of free play at the tip of the clutch release lever, as shown in **FIG 5:2**. Loosen the locknut 1 and turn the adjusting bolt 2 until the clearance is as specified, then tighten the locknut. Check the clutch cable for movement and for damage at either end fitting.

5:3 Removing and dismantling clutch

Refer to **FIG 5:3**. Loosen the release lever locknut and loosen the adjusting bolt so that maximum play is achieved at the release lever. Hold the clutch cable, remove the rubber cushion 1 from the release lever and separate the clutch cable from the release lever. Separate the clutch cable from the clutch cover, as shown in **FIG 5:4**.

Remove the clutch housing cover, then release the clutch pressure plate bolts alternately and evenly, as shown in **FIG 5:5**, until the unit is free and can be removed. Pull the friction plate from the splined shaft as shown in **FIG 5:6**.

Remove the clutch drum 1 as shown in **FIG 5:7**, taking care not to damage the oil seal 2. Refer to **FIG 5:8** and remove the retracting springs 1, diaphragm setting plate 2, and fulcrum ring, followed by the pressure disc and diaphragm spring.

Extract the cotterpin from the clutch housing as shown in **FIG 5:9**, then detach the release bearing shaft and spring from the housing. Remove the circlip and push out the release bearing shaft bushing from the housing. Support the release bearing on blocks as shown in **FIG 5:10** and tap the shaft lightly with a hammer to remove the bearing.

Inspection and servicing:

Check the release lever pivot pin for excessive play. Check the clutch housing bushing for excessive wear, as this would cause vibration or rattles in operation.

Inspect the clutch drum and pressure disc for oil or grease contamination on their working surfaces. If oil or grease is present, the affected parts must be thoroughly washed in methylated spirits. It is not sufficient to wipe them with a cloth only.

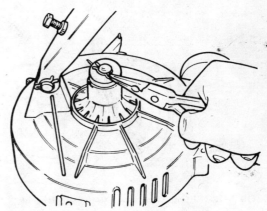

FIG 5:9 Extracting the cotter pin

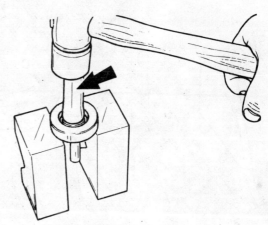

FIG 5:10 Release bearing removal

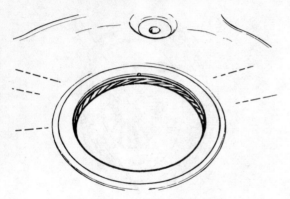

FIG 5:11   Clutch drum oil seal

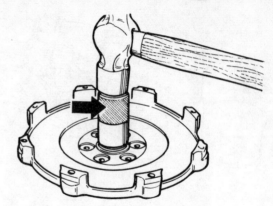

FIG 5:14   Installing the clutch drum oil seal

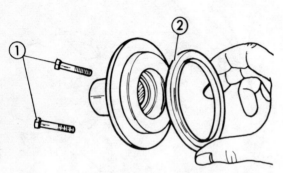

FIG 5:12   Fitting a new seal 2 to the special tool

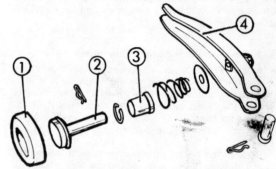

FIG 5:15   Clutch release mechanism

Key to Fig 5:15   1 Release bearing   2 Release bearing shaft   3 Bearing bushing   4 Release lever

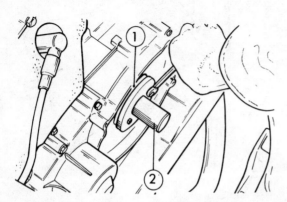

FIG 5:13   Installing the seal 1 to the housing

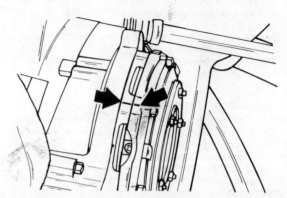

FIG 5:16   Clutch drum and pressure plate alignment

Check the drum and pressure plate working surfaces for excessive scoring or for signs of warpage. Scored surfaces may be reground at a service station, but if the wear is excessive or if the unit is warped, it must be renewed.

Check the clutch drum oil seals and, if they are worn or damaged, or if oil has been found in the clutch, renew them. Note that the 67 × 82 × 8 seal shown in **FIG 5 : 11** has helical grooves to prevent oil seepage and their presence does not indicate wear. To renew this seal, remove the old seal and fit a new seal 2 to the driver tool B as shown in **FIG 5 : 12**, applying a light coat of high melting point grease to the seal lips. Use two clutch drum mounting bolts 1 to pull the tool into position as shown in **5 : 13** and, when the seal 1 is fully seated, remove the tool. If the 20 × 30 × 5 oil seal in the drum unit is worn or damaged, remove it and fit a new seal with driver tool A, as shown in **FIG 5 : 14**, coat the seal lips with high melting point grease, then drive the seal into position.

Check the friction disc for loose rivets and worn or very loose torsional rubbers. The friction linings should be well proud of the rivets and have a light colour, through which the grain of the material is clearly visible. A polished glaze is normal, but a dark deposit indicates oil on the facings. If the friction disc linings are worn, if the unit is warped, or if it is oil contaminated, it must be renewed. Check that the friction disc hub is a smooth sliding fit on the splined shaft, removing any burrs on the shaft or in the hub. Check the release bearing by pressing it and turning it by hand. Renew the bearing if it is worn or loose in any way. Do not clean the release bearing in solvent as this would wash away the internal lubricant, wipe clean with a dry cloth only. Check the release bearing shaft and the bushing in which it operates for excessive wear.

Check the condition of the diaphragm spring and; if it is worn, damaged or weakened, renew it.

5 : 4 Assembling and refitting clutch

This is a reversal of the dismantling and removal procedures, noting the following points:

Make sure that the release bearing 1 is installed correctly on the shaft 2. The shaft should be installed from the side which has the bearing seal 3, as shown in **FIG 5 : 15**.

When installing the pressure plate assembly, be sure to align the marks on the units as shown in **FIG 5 : 16**, otherwise the balance will be lost and vibration may result.

On completion, adjust the clutch free play as described in **Section 5 : 2**.

5 : 5 Fault diagnosis

(a) Drag or spin

1 Oil or grease on friction plate linings
2 Control cable binding
3 Distorted friction plate
4 Warped or damaged pressure plate
5 Warped or damaged clutch drum
6 Broken friction linings
7 Excessive clutch free play

(b) Fierceness or snatch

1 Check 1, 2, 3 and 4 in (a)
2 Worn friction linings

(c) Slip

1 Check 1 in (a)
2 Weak diaphragm spring
3 Seized control cable
4 Insufficient clutch free play

(d) Judder

1 Check 1, 3 and 4 in (a)
2 Contact area of friction linings unevenly worn
3 Badly worn splines in friction plate hub
4 Faulty clutch drum mountings

(e) Tick or knock

1 Badly worn friction plate hub splines
2 Worn release bearing
3 Loose clutch drum
4 Worn clutch housing bushing

NOTES

CHAPTER 6

MANUAL TRANSMISSION

6:1 Description

The transmission assembly, housed in unit with the engine, is of the constant mesh type and provided with four forward speeds plus reverse. Power from the engine crankshaft is transmitted through the primary chain and sprockets to the clutch assembly, then from the clutch to the gearbox through the transmission input shaft. From the gearbox, power flow is through the differential assembly to the drive shafts which turn the front road wheels.

Each gearwheel on the mainshaft and countershaft is in constant mesh with its matching gear, the assembly being shown in the neutral position in FIG 6:1. Gearshifting is accomplished by the movement of gear dogs 2 in the manner illustrated in FIG 6:2, which lock onto the appropriate gear B or C as it is selected by shift fork 3.

No routine maintenance is required on the gearbox or differential components and lubrication is by means of the engine oil.

6:2 Gearbox servicing

The engine and transmission assembly must be removed from the car as described in Chapter 1, to provide the necessary access to the gearbox components.

Gear assembly removal:

Remove the crankcase right side cover. Straighten the lockwasher shown in FIG 6:3 and remove the bolt. Remove the reverse shift fork 2 together with reverse gear 3, as shown in FIG 6:4.

Separate the lower crankcase from the upper crankcase as described in Chapter 1, Section 1:10.

Remove the mainshaft assembly from the upper crankcase, the components of which are shown in FIG 6:5. Remove the external circlip from the mainshaft and detach reverse gear 1 from the shaft 9. Remove the set ring and detach the needle bearing retainer 2. Unfasten the needle bearing ring and remove the needle bearing 7. Remove the mainshaft top gear 8 with the two thrust plates 3 and 4. Remove the third and top shift gear 5, followed by third gear 6 and the set ring.

Separate the countershaft, shown in FIG 6:6, from the upper crankcase. Unfasten the left needle bearing retaining set ring, then remove the left needle bearing retainer and bearing. Remove the countershaft low gear 9 and the thrust plate A8. Remove the low and second shift gear 7, unfasten the external circlip and remove the thrust plate 6 and second gear 5. No attempt should be made to remove the countershaft reverse gear 1 as it is press-fitted to the shaft.

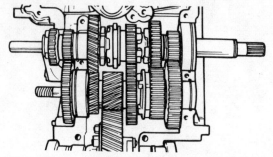

FIG 6:1 The transmission gears in the neutral position

Inspection

Inspect all gears for worn or chipped teeth, circlips and thrust plates for damage or distortion and bearings for wear, roughness or damage. Renew any faulty parts.

Measure the clearance between the needle roller bearing and the mainshaft top gear as shown in **FIG 6:7** and between the needle roller bearing and the countershaft low gear, using feeler gauges. In both cases the clearance should be between 0.15 and 0.20mm (0.0059 and 0.0079in). If the clearance exceeds 0.4mm (0.0158in), the thrust plate C in the case of the mainshaft or thrust plate A for the countershaft must be changed. Measure the thickness of the existing thrust plate and calculate the thickness needed to bring the clearance to within

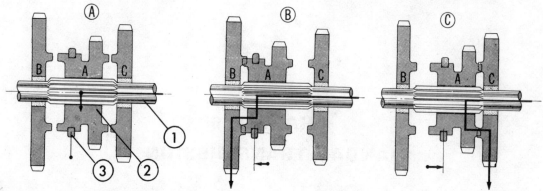

FIG 6:2 Movement of the gearshift dog to engage transmission gears

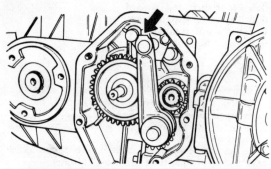

FIG 6:3 Removing the reverse shift fork bolt

FIG 6:4 Removing the reverse shift fork 2 and reverse gear 3

specifications. Thrust plates are available in three thicknesses, 1.50, 1.75 and 2.00mm.

Measure the side clearance of the mainshaft third gear. To do this, measure the clearance of the gear cotter within the mainshaft groove, using a feeler gauge as shown in **FIG 6:8**. This measurement should be between 0.2 and 0.3mm (0.0079 and 0.0118in). Renew parts if the clearance exceeds 0.5mm (0.0197in).

Measure the clearance between mainshaft top and third gears and the shaft and between the countershaft low and second gears and the shaft. To do this, use an inside micrometer to measure the bore in the gears, as shown in **FIG 6:9**. Use a standard micrometer to measure the diameter of the appropriate shaft where the gear operates, then calculate the running clearance. In all cases, clearance should be between 0.02 and 0.06mm (0.0008 and 0.0024in). If any clearance exceeds 0.1mm (0.0039in), renew parts as necessary to correct.

Check the movement between the shift gear and the splines as shown in **FIG 6:10**, renewing parts as necessary if excessive play can be felt.

On the third and top and the low and second gearshift dogs, measure the width of the side teeth as shown in **FIG 6:11**, using vernier calipers. For the top and third shift gear, renew the unit if any tooth on the third gear side has a width less than 9.6mm (0.3780in) or any on the top gear side has a width less than 9.4mm (0.3701in). Renew the low and second shift gear if any tooth has a width less than 9.2mm (0.3622in).

Check the end float of the right and left bearings on both mainshaft and countershaft, as shown in

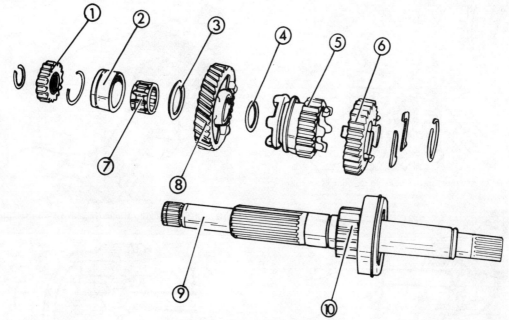

FIG 6:5   Mainshaft components

Key to Fig 6:5   1 Reverse gear   2 Bearing retainer   3 Thrust plate C   4 Thrust plate B   5 Third/top shift gear   6 Third gear
7 Needle roller bearing   8 Top gear   9 Mainshaft   10 Low gear

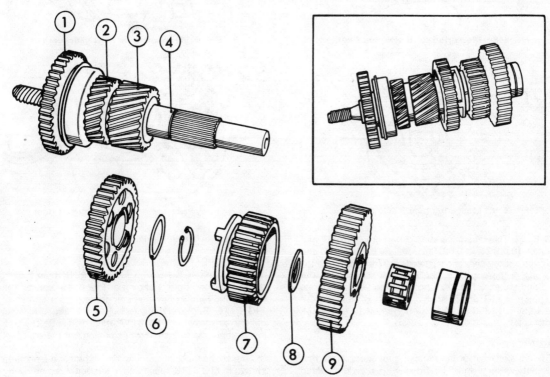

FIG 6:6   Countershaft components

Key to Fig 6:6   1 Reverse gear   2 Top gear   3 Final drive gear   4 Countershaft   5 Second gear   6 Thrust plate   7 Low/
second shift gear   8 Thrust plate A   9 Low gear

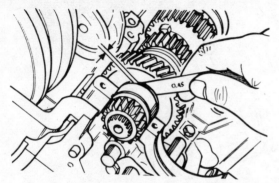

FIG 6:7   Measuring the bearing to gear clearance

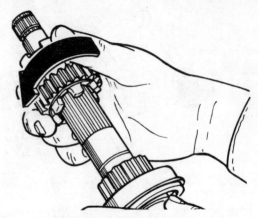

FIG 6:10   Checking the shift gear fit on the splines

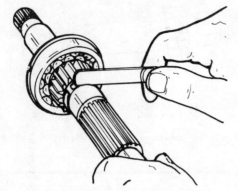

FIG 6:8   Measuring third gear end float

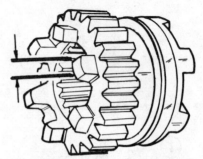

FIG 6:11   Measuring shift gear teeth

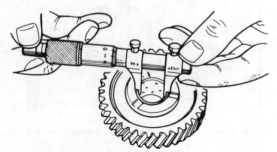

FIG 6:9   Measuring gear inside diameter

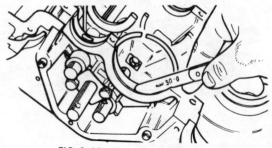

FIG 6:12   Checking bearing end float

FIG 6:12. This clearance should be between 0.03 and 0.05mm (0.0012 and 0.0020in). Renew the bearings and snap rings if the clearance exceeds 0.07mm (0.0028in).

Measure the widths of the low and second and the third and top gearshift fork fingers, using vernier calipers as shown in **FIG 6:13**. Standard width is between 4.7 and 4.8mm (0.1850 and 0.1890in). Renew the forks if the width is less than 4.6mm (0.1811in).

Refitting:

This is a reversal of the removal procedure. Note that the shaft washers must be fitted with their chamfered sides towards the fillets on the shafts, as shown in **FIG 6:14**. Lubricate the moving parts with engine oil and check for free rotation of the gears at all stages.

6:3 Gearshift mechanism

Dismantling:

Loosen the lockplates on the shift forks, then loosen the fork locking bolts 1 shown in **FIG 6:15**. Loosen the setbolt and remove the interlock guide plate 1 shown in **FIG 6:16**. Remove the interlock pin 1 and two steel balls 2 as shown in **FIG 6:17**, then dismantle the top, low and reverse fork shaft while pulling out the shift fork shaft.

Loosen the lockball spring retaining bolt at the position shown in **FIG 6:18**, then remove the bolt, washer, spring and steel ball. In a similar manner, remove the lockball assembly shown in **FIG 6:19**. Unscrew the spring seat 1 setbolts shown in **FIG 6:20** and remove the spring seat

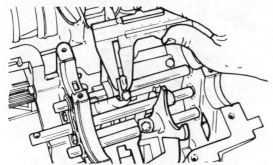

FIG 6:13 Measuring the width of the shift fork fingers

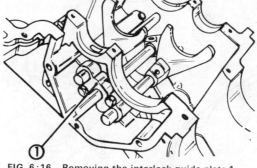

FIG 6:16 Removing the interlock guide plate 1

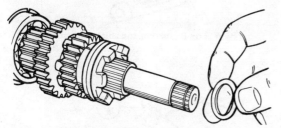

FIG 6:14 Fitting a shaft washer

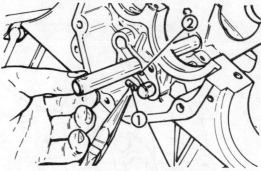

FIG 6:17 The interlock pin 1 and steel ball 2

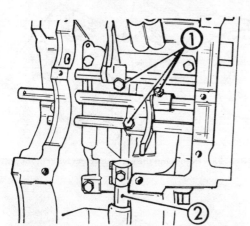

FIG 6:15 The shift fork locking bolts 1

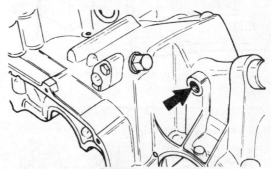

FIG 6:18 Removing the first lockball assembly

and gasket, followed by the reverse gear pin spring and the restriction pin.

Loosen the lockwasher and remove the shift arm 2 setbolt shown in **FIG 6:15**. Pull out the gearshift rod and dismantle the gearshift arm, oil seal seat and oil seal. Remove the gearshift guide plate bolts shown in **FIG 6:21**, then remove the guide plate assembly from the lower crankcase.

Remove the shift plate setscrews shown in **FIG 6:22**, then remove the reverse select lever pivot bolt 1 shown in **FIG 6:23**. Dismantle the gearshift guide lower plate, then dismantle the stopper ball spring retainer, the stopper ball pressure spring and the steel ball. **FIG 6:24** shows the three shift plates.

Reassembly:

After inspecting the parts and renewing any found worn or damaged, reassemble the gearshift mechanism in the reverse order of dismantling. Tighten the lockball spring retaining bolts shown in **FIGS 6:18** and **6:19** to a torque of 3 to 4kgm (21.7 to 28.9lb ft).

6:4 Gearshift lever and rod

FIG 6:25 shows the layout of the gearshift lever 1 and rod 3. The rod is disconnected from the lower joint by driving out the pin shown in **FIG 6:26**, this being facilitated by placing the lever in the first gear position. The shift lever bracket is attached by four bolts as shown in **FIG 6:27** and can be moved for adjustment.

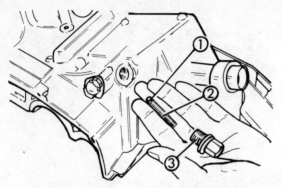

FIG 6:19   Removing the second lockball assembly

Key to Fig 6:19   1 Lockball   2 Spring   3 Cap

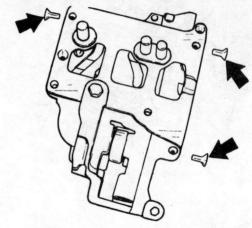

FIG 6:22   Removing the shift plate screws

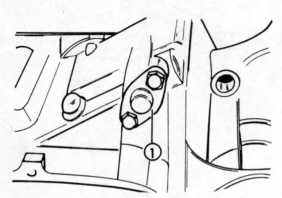

FIG 6:20   The spring seat 1 mounting

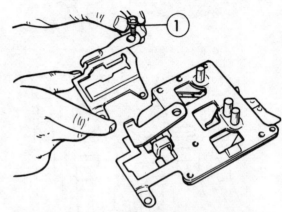

FIG 6:23   Removing the reverse select lever pivot bolt 1

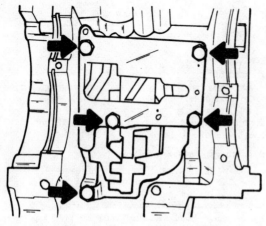

FIG 6:21   Guide plate removal

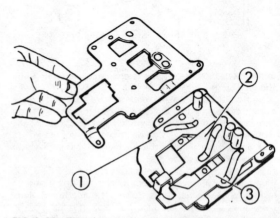

FIG 6:24   The reverse plate 1, Low/second plate 2 and third/top plate 3

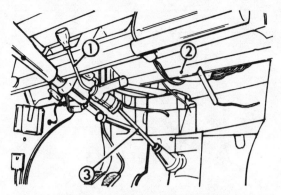

FIG 6:25   Layout of the gearshift lever 1 and rod 3

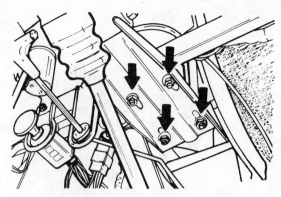

FIG 6:27   Shift lever mounting bracket

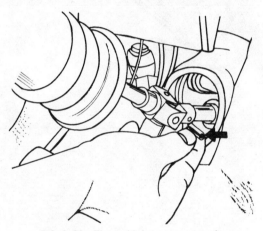

FIG 6:26   The rod joint connector pin

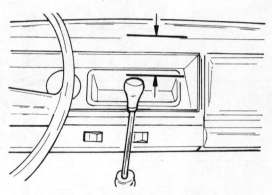

FIG 6:28   Gearshift lever positioning

Maintenance and adjustments:

The gearshift rod universal joints should be lubricated occasionally, by pulling back the rubber boots to expose the joints, cleaning them and applying a coating of grease.

Shift lever adjustment:

When the shift lever is in the first or third gear position, the distance between the grip and the instrument panel pad should be between 50 and 70mm (2.0 to 2.8in), as shown in **FIG 6:28**, this being the standard position. The lever can, however, be adjusted to a position to suit the driver. Adjustment is by means of the bracket shown in **FIG 6:27**.

Checking lever play:

Set the gearshift lever to the neutral position, then move to the left and right as shown in **FIG 6:29** and check that the play is between 50 and 60mm (2.0 to 2.4in). Play in excess of the figure stated means that the universal joints are worn and that the shift lever assembly should be renewed, no repairs being possible.

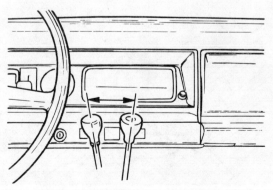

FIG 6:29   Gearshift lever play in neutral

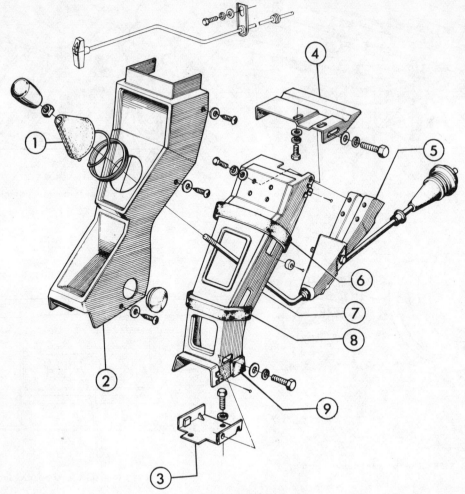

FIG 6:30 Floor shift mechanism

Key to Fig 6:30 1 Dust cover   2 Console   3 Lower bracket   4 Upper bracket   5 Lever assembly   6 Padding   7 Lever bracket   8 Padding   9 Padding

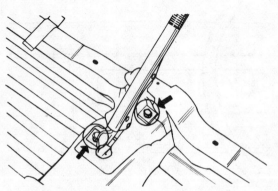

FIG 6:31 Parking brake lever bolts

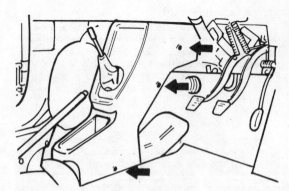

FIG 6:32 The console fastening screws

6:5 Floor shift mechanism

This type of mechanism is fitted to N600G models and is shown in **FIG 6:30**. The gearshift mechanism is, however, similar to other N series cars in all other respects.

Dismantling:

To simplify removal of the console, remove the two bolts shown in **FIG 6:31** which secure the parking brake lever and lay the assembly to one side. Remove the knob from the gearlever, then remove the six screws shown in **FIG 6:32**, three each side, which attach the console. The console can then be removed. Remove the bolts shown in **FIG 6:33** and remove the gearshift lever bracket from the floor.

Reassembly is a reversal of the removal operation.

6:6 The differential assembly

The helical gear-type differential unit is driven directly by the final drive gear, which is an integral part of the transmission countershaft. The differential assembly is enclosed in the crankcase together with the transmission and lubricated by the engine oil. **FIG 6:34** shows the differential assembly.

Dismantling:

The differential assembly should be dismantled into the order shown in **FIG 6:35**, then the components cleaned and inspected and any part found worn or damaged renewed.

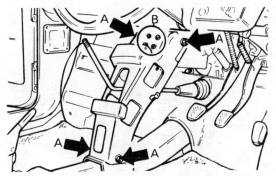

FIG 6:33 The gearshift lever bracket bolts, A = 12mm head bolts, B = 10mm head bolts

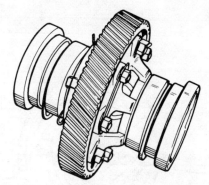

FIG 6:34 The differential assembly

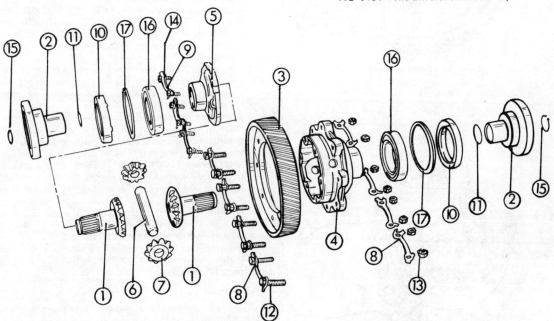

FIG 6:35 Differential components

Key to Fig 6:35 1 Differential side gear   2 Joint flange   3 Final driven gear   4 Differential gear case   5 Differential gear case cap   6 Differential pinion gearshaft   7 Pinion gear   8 Lockplate   9 Lockplate   10 Oil seal (54 × 75 × 12)   11 'O' ring 12 Setting bolt   13 Setting nut   14 Setting bolt   15 Circlip   16 Ballbearing   17 Thrust plate

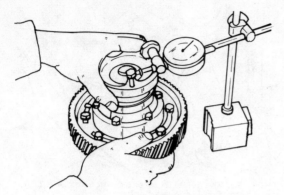

FIG 6:36 Checking backlash

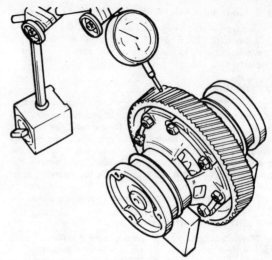

FIG 6:39 Checking ring gear eccentricity

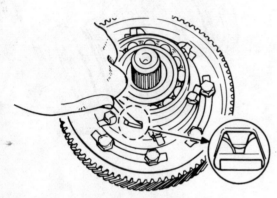

FIG 6:37 Checking pinion gear side clearance

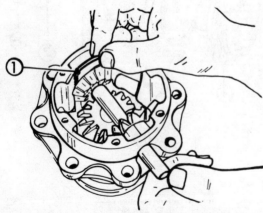

FIG 6:38 Fitting shims 1 to the pinion gear

Inspection:

Check the backlash by locking the ring gear and one side of the joint flange and measure with a dial gauge, as shown in **FIG 6:36**. Backlash should be between 0.1 and 0.4mm (0.0039 to 0.0158in) and if greater, carry out the following operations:

1 Check the wear on the splines of the differential side gear, and if found to be excessive, renew the component. Check the pinion gear side clearance with feeler gauges, as shown in **FIG 6:37**. This clearance should be between 0.1 and 0.2mm (0.0039 and 0.0079in). If greater than 0.3mm (0.0118in), install shims 1 to correct the clearance as shown in **FIG 6:38**.

2 Rotate the ring gear and check the entire circumference for concentricity. If any fault is found in this respect, remove the ring gear from the differential case and remount it correctly.

3 Check the clearance between the differential pinion shaft and pinion. Measure the shaft diameter and the pinion inside diameter with a micrometer and calculate the working clearance. This should be between 0.03 and 0.09mm (0.0012 and 0.0035in). Renew parts as necessary if the clearance exceeds 0.15mm (0.0059in).

4 Measure the eccentricity of the differential gear. Support the bearings on V-blocks and measure the eccentricity in four places, turning the gear 90° each time, as shown in **FIG 6:39**. If eccentricity exceeds 0.1mm (0.0039in), loosen the gear retaining bolt and adjust by tapping carefully with a soft-faced hammer. If this procedure does not improve matters, the gear must be renewed.

Assembly:

This is a reversal of the dismantling procedure, noting the following points:

Check that the differential side gear 'O' ring is in good condition, renewing it if not. Assemble the ring gear into the differential case, then tighten the mounting bolts shown in **FIG 6:40** to 2.8 to 3.0kgm (20.25 to 21.70lb ft).

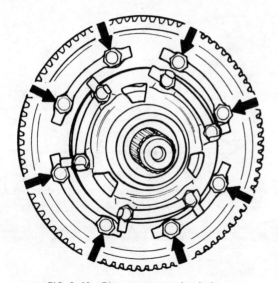

FIG 6:40 Ring gear mounting bolts

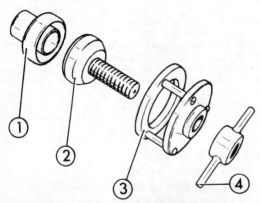

FIG 6:41 The special tool needed for differential oil seal renewal

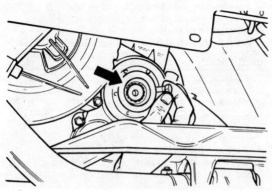

FIG 6:42 Differential joint flange removal

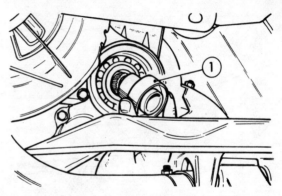

FIG 6:43 Fitting part 1 of the special tool

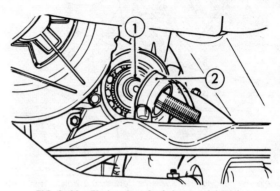

FIG 6:44 Fitting part 2 of the special tool

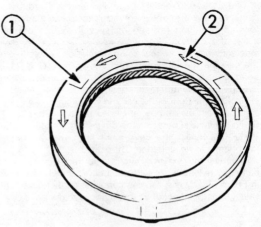

FIG 6:45 The oil seal identification marks

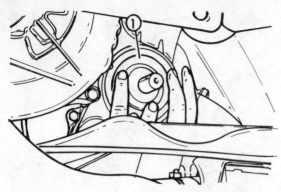

FIG 6:46 Fitting the oil seal 1 to the special tool

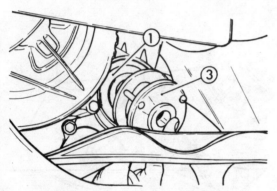

FIG 6:47 Fitting part 3 of the special tool

Always use new lockwashers under the bolt heads and bend them over the heads to retain the bolts. Make sure that differential oil seals are in good condition and properly mounted against the bearings. Renew them if defective in any way.

6:7 Differential oil seal renewal

With the differential assembly removed from the crankcase and dismantled, oil seal renewal is a straightforward operation needing no special tools. However, using the method described in this section for seal renewal when the engine and transmission is installed in the car, the special Honda tool shown in FIG 6:41 is essential. Seal renewal is necessary to correct any oil leakage from the differential gear.

Jack up the front of the car and safely support on floor stands. Drain the engine oil as described in Chapter 1. Clean the linkage between the drive shaft and differential shaft. Disconnect the drive shaft from the differential joint flange as described in Chapter 8.

Remove the external circlip and remove the joint flange by pulling it out with the bolt attached, as shown in FIG 6:42. Have a suitable container ready to catch oil spillage that may occur as the flange is removed.

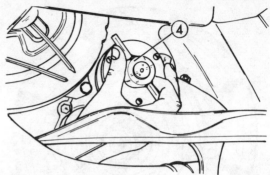

FIG 6:48 Pressing the seal into place with the special tool 4

Use a puller to draw out the defective seal, then check that no seal internal springs have been left in the differential gear case. Use a piece of thin wire to relocate the 'O' ring on the side gear. This 'O' ring must be adjacent to the spline.

Insert part 1 of the special tool into the side gear as shown in FIG 6:43 and securely fit the external circlip. Thread part 2 of the tool into part 1, as shown in FIG 6:44. Ensure that the correct seal has been obtained, noting the L or R mark to denote left or right side of the car and the arrow marks indicating the direction of rotation, as shown in FIG 6:45.

Fit the seal 1 to the tool as shown in FIG 6:46, greasing the outside of the seal to ease fitting. Attach part 3 of the tool as shown in FIG 6:47. Thread the handle 4 (see FIG 6:48) of the special tool into place and tighten to force the seal into position. When the seal is fully home remove the tool and refit the external circlip securely. Refit the remaining parts in the reverse order of removal.

6:8 Fault diagnosis

(a) Jumping out of gear

1 Excessively worn selector mechanism
2 Worn gearshift dog teeth
3 Loose or worn selector fork

(b) Noisy transmission

1 Insufficient oil
2 Bearings worn or damaged
3 Worn drive shaft joints
4 Worn gears or shafts
5 Worn or damaged differential components

(c) Difficulty in engaging gear

1 Incorrect clutch adjustment
2 Worn gearshift dog units
3 Worn selector shafts or forks

(d) Oil leaks

1 Damaged joint washers or gaskets
2 Worn or damaged oil seals
3 Faulty joint faces on crankcase components

CHAPTER 7

AUTOMATIC TRANSMISSION

7:1 Description

The Hondamatic automatic transmission is supplied as an optional extra to take the place of the usual clutch and gearbox. A cut-away view of the automatic transmission and differential is shown in **FIG 7:1**. The transmission utilises a torque converter and a constant mesh gear set, with three clutches and the necessary control valves, to provide three forward speeds and reverse. Automatic gearchanges are controlled by road speed, engine load and throttle position.

The torque converter shown in **FIG 7:2** consists of an impeller, turbine, stator and one-way clutch. When the engine is running, crankshaft rotation is transmitted directly to the impeller shaft. As the impeller revolves, the fluid in the torque converter housing transmits power to the turbine by flowing in a spiral pattern as shown in **FIG 7:3**. The stator re-directs the flow of fluid as it leaves the turbine so that it re-enters the impeller at the most effective angle.

When the engine is idling, the converter impeller is being driven slowly and the energy of the fluid leaving it is low, so little torque is imparted to the turbine. For this reason, with the engine idling and drive engaged, the car will have little or no tendency to 'creep'. As the throttle is opened the impeller speed increases and the process of torque multiplication begins. As the turbine picks up speed and the slip between it and the impeller becomes less, the torque multiplication reduces progressively until, when their speeds become substantially equal, the unit acts as a fluid coupling. In this condition the stator is no longer required to re-direct the fluid and the one-way clutch permits it to rotate with the impeller and turbine.

Power flow through the automatic transmission is as follows:

Power from the engine crankshaft is passed to the input side of the impeller shaft through a splined collar connection, the impeller rotating at engine speed. The turbine shaft turns the primary drive sprocket which drives the automatic gearbox through the primary chain and driven sprocket. The impeller and turbine shafts are concentric, as shown in **FIG 7:4**. The final drive gear in the automatic gearbox directly drives the differential unit, which, in turn, transmits power through the drive shafts to the front wheels.

7:2 Servicing procedures

The maintenance, adjustment and testing procedures which can be carried out by a reasonably competent

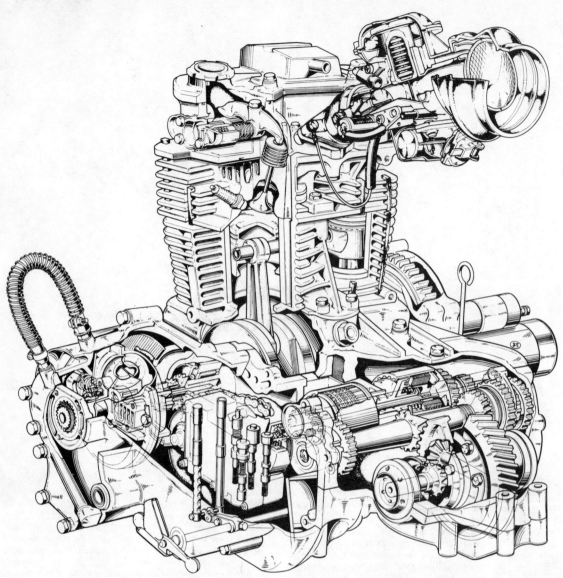

FIG 7:1   Cut-away view of the automatic transmission and differential

owner are given in this chapter. More serious performance faults which require pressure take-off points to be opened and pressure measurements taken for test purposes, adjustment of hydraulic components or partial or complete dismantling to replace worn or damaged components dictate that the services of a fully equipped specialist be enlisted.

Due to the need for removal and dismantling of several major transmission components to gain access to the engine primary drive train and crankshaft assemblies, servicing of these components, as well as transmission overhaul work, should be carried out by qualified personnel at a Honda service station.

Transmission removal:

The automatic transmission is removed from the car in unit with the engine, in a similar manner to that described in **Chapter 1** for manual transmission models. However, certain extra components must be disconnected, as described in the following paragraphs. **FIG 7:5** shows the installation of the engine and automatic transmission in the car.

Loosen the locknut 1 and detach the secondary cable 4 from the carburetter, as shown in **FIG 7:6**. Loosen the locknuts on the selector cables A1 and B5, as shown in **FIG 7:7**, then disconnect the cables from the selector

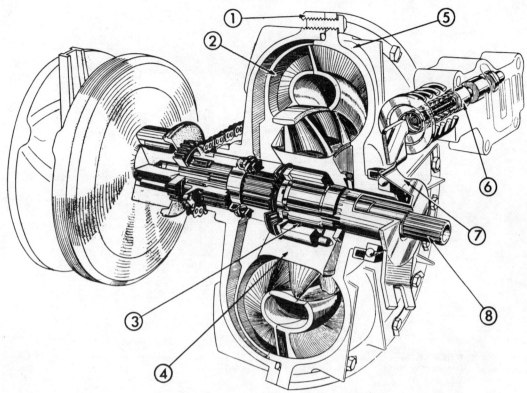

FIG 7:2 Cut-away view of the torque converter

Key to Fig 7:2 1 Converter housing   2 Impeller   3 One-way clutch   4 Stator   5 Turbine   6 Pressure regulator valve
7 Regulator valve operating arm   8 Shaft

strap arm 3. Disconnect the cables A2 and B1 from the manual select lever 3, as shown in **FIG 7:8**.

To disconnect the exhaust system, loosen the clamp retaining nut at the tail end of the manifolds, remove the bolt and release the clamp plate 2 on the converter cover 1, then separate the exhaust manifold from the cylinder head (see **FIG 7:9**). There is no need to remove the exhaust manifolds from the engine compartment.

Separate the transmission oil cooler 2 from the front of the engine compartment 1, as shown in **FIG 7:10**.

Refitting is carried out in the reverse order of removal. On completion, check and adjust the throttle cable, the throttle secondary cable and the selector cables A and B.

Check the level of fluid in the automatic transmission and carry out operational tests to ensure proper operation.

7:3 Maintenance

The automatic transmission fluid level should be checked at 5000km (3000 mile) intervals. At 20,000km (12,000 mile) intervals the fluid should be drained and the transmission filled with new fluid of the correct type, which is good quality ATF type A. **Never use anything but the correct type of fluid in the automatic transmission.**

Whenever operational faults occur, the fluid level should be checked first, followed by checks on the throttle secondary cable and selector cable adjustments.

Checking fluid level:

This operation must be carried out with the fluid warm after a short run, the engine running at idling speed and the transmission in the 3 position. The handbrake should be fully applied and, additionally, the road wheels should be chocked or the footbrake applied by an assistant, to ensure that there is no possibility of the car moving forward. Under these conditions, remove the transmission dipstick, wipe it with a clean, lint-free cloth,

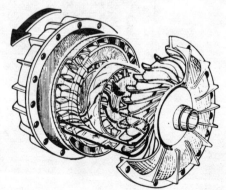

FIG 7:3   Fluid flow through the torque converter

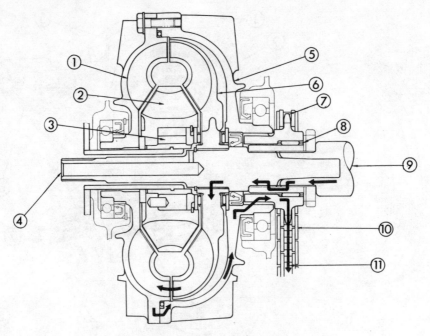

FIG 7:4 Power flow through the torque converter

Key to Fig 7:4 1 Turbine 2 Stator 3 One-way clutch 4 Shaft 5 Casing 6 Impeller 7 Primary drive sprocket 8 Coupling 9 Crankshaft 10 Primary drive chain 11 Power flow

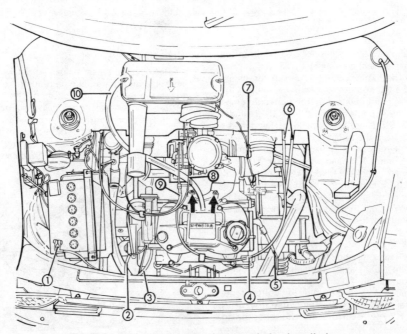

FIG 7:5 Engine and automatic transmission installation

Key to Fig 7:5 1 Negative terminal 2 Ignition primary lead 3 Engine earth cable 4 Throttle secondary cable 5 HT cable 6 Selector cables 7 Fuel solenoid valve lead 8 Choke cable 9 Throttle cable 10 Breather tube

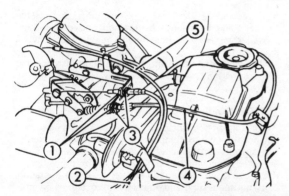

FIG 7:6 Disconnecting the throttle secondary cable

Key to Fig 7:6 1 Locknuts 2 Throttle cable 3 Adjusting nuts 4 Throttle secondary cable 5 Choke cable

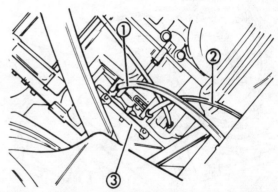

FIG 7:8 Disconnecting the cables from the selector lever

Key to Fig 7:8 1 Selector cable B 2 Selector cable A 3 Manual control lever

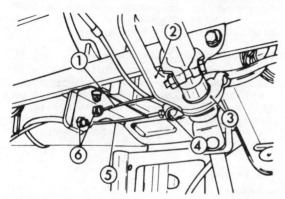

FIG 7:7 Disconnecting the cables from the selector strap arm

Key to Fig 7:7 1 Selector cable A 2 Selector strap 3 Arm 4 Cable end ball 5 Selector cable B 6 Adjusting nuts

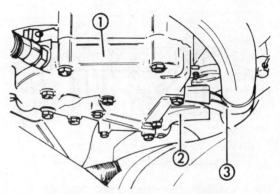

FIG 7:9 Detaching the exhaust system

Key to Fig 7:9 1 Torque converter casing cover 2 Exhaust manifold clamp B 3 Exhaust manifold clamp A

replace it and remove again to take the reading. The fluid level should be between the marks on the dipstick. If not, add fluid through the dipstick hole until the correct level is reached. The difference between the two marks corresponds to an additional half Imp. pint. **FIG 7:11** shows the location of the dipstick 1 and the fluid level markings (inset).

Changing transmission fluid:

When the transmission is warm after a run, remove the drain plug 3 shown in **FIG 7:12** and allow the fluid to drain into a suitable container. Check the old fluid at this stage, as a dark colour and burnt smell can indicate a burned internal clutch plate which needs specialist attention.

After all fluid has drained, refit the drain plug and add new automatic transmission fluid up to the top mark on the dipstick. Normally, approximately 1.7 litres (3 Imp. pints) will be needed to refill the transmission. The total

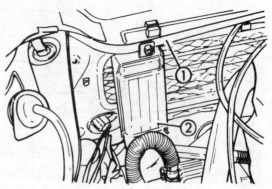

FIG 7:10 The transmission oil cooler 2 at the front bulkhead 1

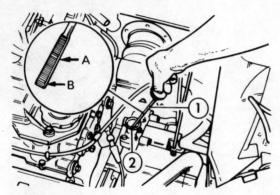

FIG 7:11 Transmission dipstick 1 and fluid level markings. A is the upper limit, B is the lower limit and 2 the filler neck

FIG 7:12 The automatic transmission fluid drain plug 3. 1 is the oil drain plug and 2 the filter bolt

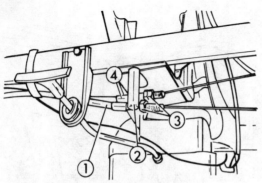

FIG 7:13 Selector cable adjustment

Key to Fig 7:13 1 Selector cable A 2 Control cable bracket 3 Adjusting nuts 4 Selector cable B

fluid capacity is 3.2 litres (5.6 Imp. pints) but, as the torque converter cannot be drained and certain fluid passages remain full, less fluid is required at renewal stages.

On completion, drive the car for a short distance and recheck the fluid level.

7:4 Cable adjustments

The adjustments given in this section should be carried out occasionally to compensate for any cable stretch in service and, additionally, whenever gearchange faults are noted. If such faults are not cured by this procedure, or if the cables are being refitted after a service operation, carry out the testing and adjustment procedures given in **Section 7:5**.

Selector cable adjustment:

Place the selector lever in the P position and adjust the white cable A1, shown in **FIG 7:13**, so that the slack is just taken up. Now place the selector lever in the 1 position and carry out similar adjustments to the black cable B4. Hold the adjuster nut 3 while retightening the locknut, to prevent altering the adjustment.

Throttle secondary cable adjustment:

Open the throttle arm lever 1 fully by hand, as shown in **FIG 7:14**, then check for slack in the secondary throttle cable by opening the carburetter throttle valve fully. If any slack exists in the cable, correct by adjusting at the point 1 shown in **FIG 7:15**. Hold the adjusting nut while retightening the locknut, to prevent altering the adjustment.

7:5 Testing

Roat test:

Drive the car over a suitable route so that the full performance of the transmission can be assessed. All gearchanges should be made quickly and without interrupting the power flow. Listen for any sign of engine run-up or increase in speed during changes, which would indicate a slipping internal clutch.

On a level road, accelerate the car from rest on full throttle and check the points on the speedometer at which gearchanges occur. On 360 models, upchanges should occur at the approximate speeds of 35km/hr (22 mile/hr) and 65km/hr (40 mile/hr). On 600 models, upchanges should occur at the approximate speeds of 42km/hr (26 mile/hr) and 80km/hr (50 mile/hr). If necessary, make adjustments in the following manner. Note that it is not possible to adjust the 1st–2nd gearchange point without changing the 2nd–3rd gearchange point as well, and vice versa. If the interval between the two gearchanges is too great after adjustment, the valve body assembly must be changed to correct the condition, this being a specialist job.

To adjust the gearchange points, act on the adjustment nuts at the throttle secondary cable. To delay the gearchange points, tighten the nuts to shorten the inner cable; to bring forward the gearchange points, loosen the nuts. Make adjustments a little at a time and test at each stage to check the setting.

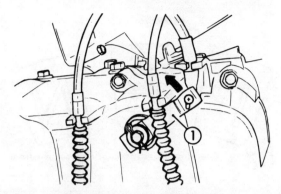

FIG 7:14   The throttle arm lever 1

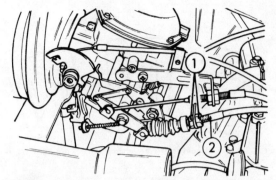

FIG 7:15   Throttle secondary cable 2 and adjustment nuts 1

Setting the selector cables:

Position the selector lever 1 in the car so that the indicator 3 is pointing to the N mark on the quadrant 2. Now position the control lever 12 on the transmission to the neutral range, as shown in **FIG 7:16**. The punch mark on the drive arm shaft 11, the mark on the control lever 12 and the N mark on the case should all be aligned.

Connect the lower ends of the selector cables A8 and B9 to their respective points on the control lever 12, applying a little grease to the ball end connectors. Connect the upper ends of the cables to the hooks on the selector strap hooks at the selector lever 4. Adjust the cables at the adjustment nuts 6 until slack is just removed from both, then loosen the adjustment nuts by half a turn each. Hold the nuts while tightening the locknuts 7 to avoid changing the settings.

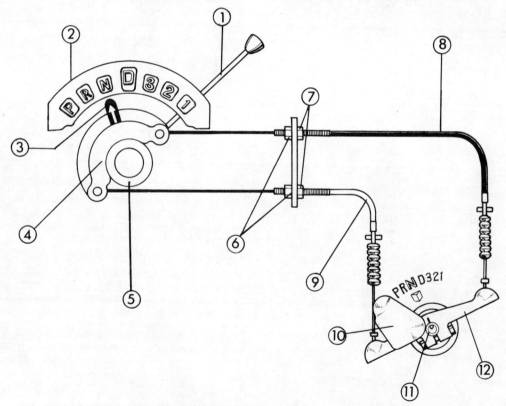

FIG 7:16   Setting the transmission and selector mechanism in neutral

Key to Fig 7:16   1 Selector lever   2 Indicator plate   3 Indicator   4 Strap lever   5 Selector strap   6 Adjusting nuts   7 Locknuts   8 Selector cable A   9 Selector cable B   10 Cam   11 Drive arm shaft   12 Control lever

FIG 7:17 Checking the selection of reverse gear from neutral

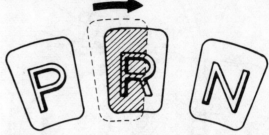

FIG 7:18 Checking the selection of reverse gear from park position

Gear selection tests:

Carry out the cable adjustments described in **Section 7:4**. Move the selector through all ranges and check that the gears engage properly. Check that, when the car is parked on a slight incline with P selected and the brakes released, the parking pawl in the transmission holds the car firmly against movement.

With the engine running and the brakes applied, check the gear selections in the following manner:

Move the selector lever from the N position towards the R position slowly. The gearchange should occur when the indicator has moved one-third of the way into the R window on the quadrant, as shown in **FIG 7:17**. In a similar manner, check that the transmission moves into the park position from reverse when the indicator is one-third of the way into the P window. Now move the selector from park position back to reverse and check that the gearchange occurs when the indicator is two-thirds of the way into the R window (see **FIG 7:18**).

To make a final check on cable adjustment, select position 1 and check that no slack exists in cables A or B. Select position D and check that both cables A and B have 2 to 4mm (0.080 to 0.160in) of slack. The load on each cable should be 1kg (2.2lb).

CHAPTER 8

FRONT SUSPENSION AND DRIVE SHAFTS

8:1 Description

The drive shafts are bolted to the differential side flanges at the inner ends and pressed into the steering knuckles at the outer ends, two universal joints being provided at each shaft to accommodate steering and suspension movements.

The independent front suspension consists of coil springs and hydraulic dampers combined into single strut units. The struts are attached to the car bodywork at their upper ends and located at their lower ends by control arms and radius rods, except on models exported to the USA, where control arms and a stabiliser bar are employed.

No routine maintenance is required, but an occasional check should be made on the condition of the suspension ball joints and the condition of the drive shaft universal joints and sealing bellows. If a bellows is split or otherwise damaged it should be renewed, or road dirt will accelerate wear of the joint. Check the front wheel hub nuts occasionally, as described in **Section 8:2**.

8:2 Drive shafts

The front drive shaft assemblies consist of an axle shaft and a drive shaft attached by a universal joint, connected by a second universal joint to the differential flange. A constant velocity ball joint is employed for the inner joint on all models and for the outer joint also on 600 models. On 360 models, a double cross joint is used at the outer position. **FIGS 8:1** and **8:2** show the drive shaft assemblies for the 360 and 600 models respectively.

The outer ball joints on 600 models cannot be serviced at all. The double cross outer joints on 360 models require a large number of special tools and specialised knowledge in order to overhaul the components, so this work, if necessary, should be carried out by a fully equipped service station. Owner servicing, therefore, will be limited to the inner universal joint assemblies as described in this section.

In order to remove the drive shafts from the hub, a special puller tool is required. The shafts are simply disconnected from the differential flanges for engine removal, however.

Tightening hub nuts:

The front wheel hub nuts should periodically be checked for tightness, as loose hub nuts can cause shimmy or vibration and rapid bearing wear. The thread diameter may be either 20 or 22mm, but the torque required is the same in either case.

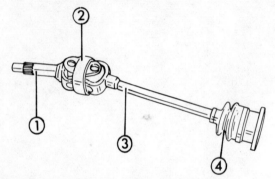

FIG 8:1 Drive shaft assembly, 360 models

Key to Fig 8:1   1 Axle shaft   2 Double cross joint
3 Drive shaft   4 Constant velocity ball joint

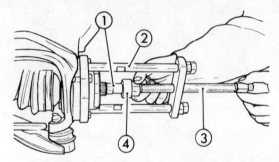

FIG 8:4   Assembling the special remover tool

Key to Fig 8:4   1 Axle shaft   2 Puller   3 Centre bolt
4 Retainer

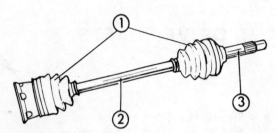

FIG 8:2   Drive shaft assembly, 600 models

Key to Fig 8:2   1 Constant velocity ball joints   2 Drive
shaft   3 Axle shaft

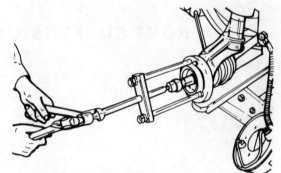

FIG 8:5   Pressing out the drive shaft

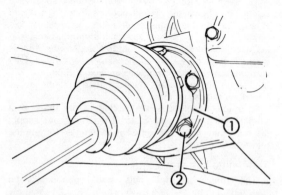

FIG 8:3 Disconnecting the drive shaft from the
differential flange

Key to Fig 8:3   1 Lockplate   2 Bolt

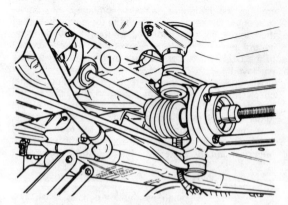

FIG 8:6   Removing the knuckle clamp bolt 1

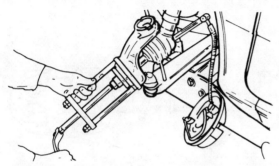

FIG 8:7 Final removal of the drive shaft with the knuckle detached

Remove the hub cap from the wheel and the cotter pin from the hub nut. Tighten the nut to a torque of 14kgm (101lb ft), then check whether the cotter pin holes in the nut and shaft are aligned. If not, tighten the nut a little further until they are aligned. If they are aligned when the correct torque figure is reached, tighten the nut through a further 30° to align the next hole in the nut. Never loosen the nut to align the cotter pin hole. Fit the cotter pin and lock.

Drive shaft removal:

Loosen the front wheel nuts, raise and safely support the front of the car, then remove the road wheels and brake drums or disc brake hubs. Refer to **Chapter 11** for details of the braking system. Remove the backing plate from the knuckle, or the dust seal cover for disc brakes. Do not disconnect the brake line, or bleeding will be necessary when the parts are reconnected.

Disconnect the drive shaft from the differential flange as shown in **FIG 8:3**, by removing the three bolts on 360 models, six bolts 2 for 600 models.

Mount the flange part of the special tool (drive shaft replacer) on the steering knuckle. Attach the other parts of the tool to the flange as shown in **FIG 8:4**, making sure that the shafts are fully threaded into the flange and that the locknuts are securely tightened. Oil the threads on the centre bolt. The special tool attachment piece must be used if the shaft has a 22mm diameter thread.

Tighten the tool centre bolt with a spanner, tapping the end of the centre bolt with a hammer while doing so, as shown in **FIG 8:5**. Take care to avoid interference of the inner end of the shaft with the engine.

When the axle shaft has been pushed about two-thirds of the way out of the knuckle, remove the knuckle from the front damper by removing the bolt 1 shown in **FIG 8:6** then tapping the knuckle downward with a soft-faced hammer. This bolt must be tightened to the correct torque when refitting, 2.8 to 3.4kgm (20 to 25lb ft) for 8mm bolt, 4.5 to 5.0kgm (33 to 36lb ft) for 10mm bolt. With the knuckle separated, tighten the tool again to fully remove the drive shaft, as shown in **FIG 8:7**.

Refitting:

This is a reversal of the removal procedure, using the special tool to pull the shaft into the steering knuckle. The inner and outer wheel bearings should be fitted as described in **Section 8:5**.

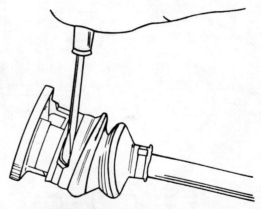

FIG 8:8 Removing the bellows band

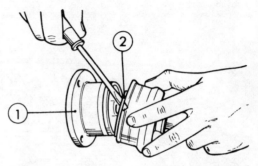

FIG 8:9 Removing the circlip 2 from the flange 1

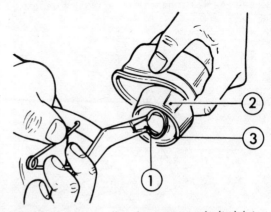

FIG 8:10 Dismantling the constant velocity joint

Key to Fig 8:10   1 Circlip   2 Steel ball   3 Retainer

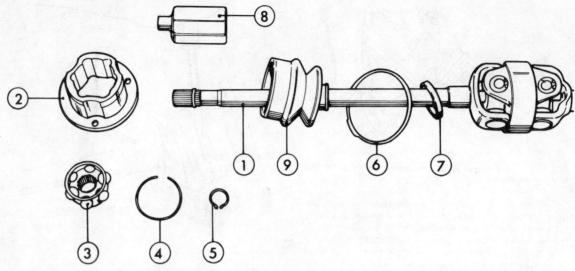

FIG 8:11   Drive shaft and constant velocity joint components

Key to Fig 8:11   1 Drive shaft   2 Flange   3 Inner ring, retainer, steel ball   4 Internal circlip   5 External circlip   6 Bellows band   7 Bellows neck band   8 Grease (50g)   9 Bellows

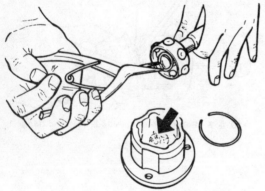

FIG 8:12   Fitting the retainer to the drive shaft

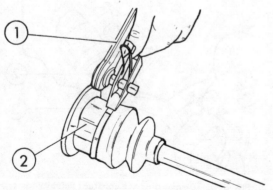

FIG 8:13   Tightening the bellows band with special tool 1

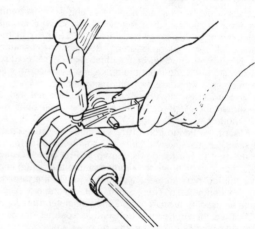

FIG 8:14   Locking the bellows band

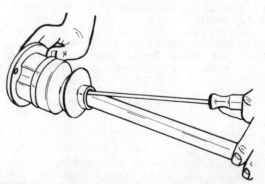

FIG 8:15   Venting the bellows for correct installation

Constant velocity joint servicing:

Dismantling:

After peeling off the end of the bellows band with pliers, remove the band by the use of a screwdriver and hammer as shown in **FIG 8:8**. Do this carefully to avoid damage to the bellows. Remove the bellows, then remove the circlip 2 from the flange 1 as shown in **FIG 8:9**. Remove the inner ring circlip 1 and withdraw the steel ball 2 and retainer 3 from the drive shaft, as shown in **FIG 8:10**. Clean all parts thoroughly and examine for wear or damage, renewing parts as necessary. **FIG 8:11** shows the drive shaft and joint components.

Assembly:

Insert the bellows neck band, bellows band and bellows onto the drive shaft. Fill the flange two-thirds full of grease. Set the steel ball in the inner ring and retainer by tapping with a soft-faced hammer. Insert the retainer into the drive shaft as shown in **FIG 8:12** and secure with the circlip.

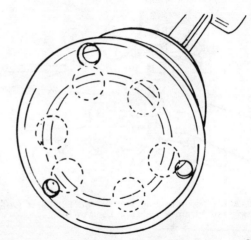

FIG 8:16 Caulking the sealing plate flange on **360** models

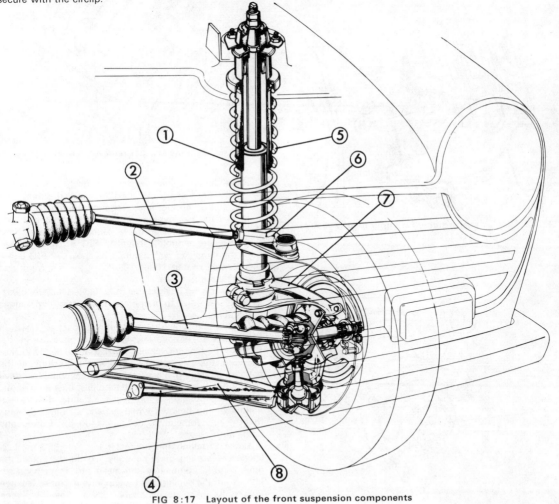

FIG 8:17 Layout of the front suspension components

Key to Fig 8:17   1 Strut   2 Tie rod   3 Drive shaft   4 Radius rod   5 Coil spring   6 Ball joint   7 Knuckle   8 Lower arm

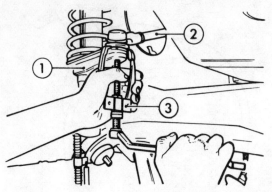

FIG 8:18 Disconnecting the tie rod ball joint with special tool 3 from knuckle arm 1 and tie rod 2

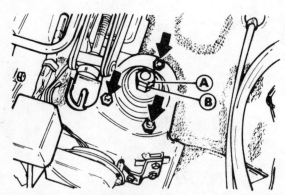

FIG 8:19 The suspension strut upper mounting nuts

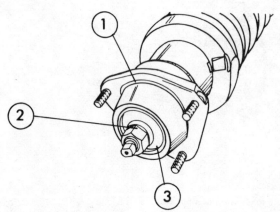

FIG 8:20 Removing the damper mounting bracket 1

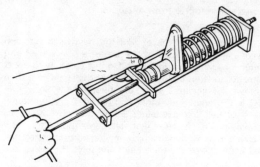

FIG 8:21 Compressing the front suspension spring

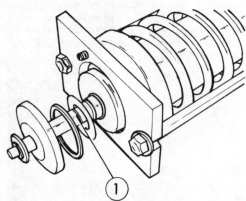

FIG 8:22 Ring stopper removal, 1 is the groove

Raise the drive shaft with the flange side down, then insert the drive shaft into the flange. Fill the joint with grease, but do not put any grease into the bellows.

Mount the bellows on the flange by aligning it with the flange peripheral groove. Tighten the bellows band with the special tool 1 shown in FIG 8:13, or similar. Lock the band end with a punch, as shown in FIG 8:14, then cut off all but 10mm (0.4in) of the band end and bend this portion over.

The following instructions must be carefully followed, as it is essential to carry out final fitting operations correctly.

Insert a thin screwdriver into the bellows as shown in FIG 8:15, to remove any vacuum or pressure inside. Remove the screwdriver and check that the bellows is not distorted, then tighten the band in this position. If the bellows projecting piece makes contact with the drive shaft when the shaft is bent to its fullest operating angle, the band is positioned too near the flange. If there is a hollow in the bellows when expanded fully, it means that the air volume in the bellows is too low. Correct any faults at this stage.

When installing the original flange on 360 models, check the sealing plate carefully. To do this, push the drive shaft in completely and make sure that no grease leaks from the sealing plate periphery. If grease leakage occurs, fix the plate periphery with a screwdriver then caulk approximately 2mm (0.08in) from the edge in six places, as shown in FIG 8:16.

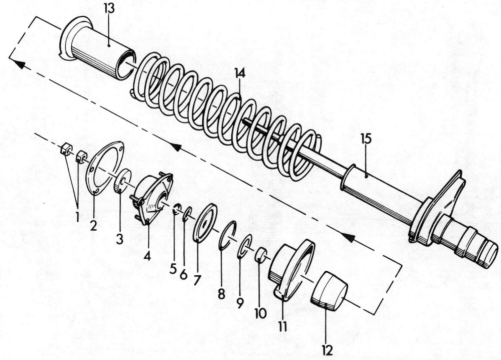

FIG 8:23 Suspension strut components

Key to Fig 8:23   1 14mm nuts   2 Mounting plate   3 Washer   4 Upper mounting bracket   5 Ring stopper   6 Washer
7 Thrust plate   8 'O' ring   9 Thrust bearing   10 Bush   11 Spring seat   12 Bump rubber   13 Dust cover   14 Coil spring
15 Damper

8:3 Suspension strut

Removal:

FIG 8:17 shows the layout of the front suspension components. Raise the front of the car and safely support on floor stands with the suspension hanging free. Disconnect the tie rod end ball joint from the steering knuckle arm 1, using a ball joint puller 3 as shown in **FIG 8:18**. Remove the steering knuckle clamp bolt shown in **FIG 8:6**, then remove the knuckle from the damper by tapping downward with a soft-faced hammer.

If the strut unit is to be dismantled after removal, loosen the two nuts shown at A and B in **FIG 8:19**, as these nuts are too tight to be removed after the damper has been detached from the car. When refitting, nut A should be tightened to 4.5 to 5.0kgm (32 to 36lb ft) and nut B to 2.5 to 3.0kgm (18 to 22lb ft).

Remove the three nuts and spring washers arrowed in **FIG 8:19** to separate the front damper from the body. When refitting, tighten these nuts to 1.5 to 2.0kgm (11 to 14lb ft).

Dismantling:

For this operation, a special spring compressing tool will be needed. Remove the damper rod nuts and washers, then remove the mounting bracket 1 shown in **FIG 8:20**. Install the front damper spring compressor and align centrally with the three adjusting screws. Turn the tool handle slowly and gradually compress the spring as shown in **FIG 8:21**.

When the spring is compressed far enough, remove the ring stopper as shown in **FIG 8:22** and release the compressor tool. The spring can then be removed.

FIG 8:23 shows the components of a standard suspension strut assembly, the modified version fitted to models exported to the USA being shown in **FIG 8:24**. The damper unit cannot be dismantled.

Reassembly and refitting the suspension strut are reversals of the dismantling and removal procedures.

8:4 Stabiliser bar (USA models)

Removal:

Raise the front of the car and support safely on floor stands so that the front suspension hangs free. Remove the castle nut 1 from each end of the stabiliser as shown in **FIG 8:25** and the two front mounting bolts 1 as shown in **FIG 8:26**, then remove the stabiliser from the car.

Refitting:

This is a reversal of the removal procedure, tightening the bolts to 2.0 to 2.4kgm (14 to 17lb ft) and the nuts to 4.5 to 5.0kgm (32 to 36lb ft). Note that the longer front support bracket should be fitted at the left side of the car, while the shorter bracket is fitted on the right.

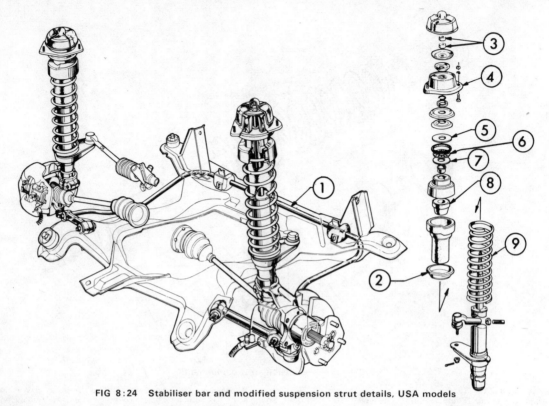

FIG 8:24   Stabiliser bar and modified suspension strut details, USA models

Key to Fig 8:24   1 Stabiliser bar   2 Spring seat   3 14mm nuts   4 Upper mounting bracket   5 Thrust plate   6 Needle roller bearing   7 Thrust plate   8 Bump rubber   9 Coil spring

8:5 Steering knuckle and lower arm

Removal:

Remove the drive shaft from the steering knuckle as described in **Section 8:2**. Pull out the lower ball joint cotter pin and remove the nut, then separate the lower arm 2 from the knuckle 1, as shown in **FIG 8:27**. Tighten the ball joint nut to 4.0 to 4.8kgm (29 to 35lb ft) when refitting.

Disconnect the radius rod 2 from the engine support beam 1 as shown in **FIG 8:28**.

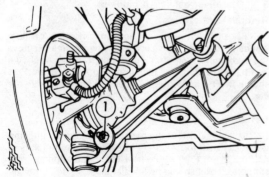

FIG 8:25   Stabiliser mounting nuts 1

Wheel bearings:

Turn the bearings in the steering knuckle with the fingers to check for wear or roughness. If faulty in any way, the bearings should be renewed. Remove the bearing cover. Place a screwdriver against the bearing and tap lightly as shown in **FIG 8:29** to remove the bearing. Two bearings are used and each must be removed from the inside. Remove the spacer fitted between the bearings, the assembly being shown in **FIG 8:30**. Fit the new bearings in the reverse order of removal, placing the bearings squarely over the bore and driving carefully into place. Use a flat plate against the bearing and tap this plate with a hammer. Tap against the outer race only, never against the inner race.

Ball joint removal:

The lower arm ball joint 1 is removed by releasing the circlip 2, shown in **FIG 8:31**, then tapping lightly with a hammer to release the joint from its mounting.

Refitting:

This is a reversal of the removal procedure. When reconnecting the radius rod to the engine mounting beam, make sure that the rubber cushions 1 are fitted at each side of the flange, as shown in **FIG 8:32**.

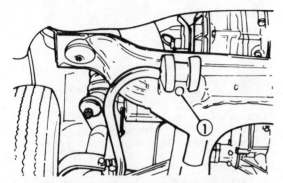

FIG 8:26 Stabiliser mounting bolts 1

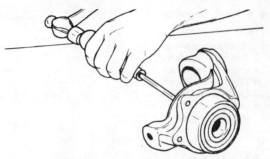

FIG 8:29 Wheel bearing removal

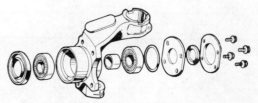

FIG 8:30 Wheel bearing assembly exploded view

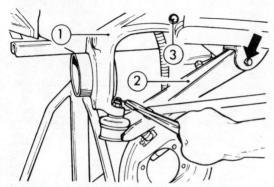

FIG 8:27 Disconnecting the lower arm 2 from the steering knuckle 1

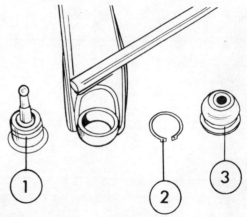

FIG 8:31 Lower arm ball joint 1 removal, 2 circlip, 3 boot

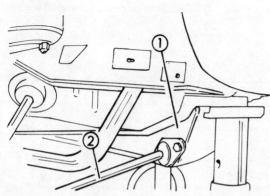

FIG 8:28 Disconnecting the radius rod 2 from the engine support beam 1

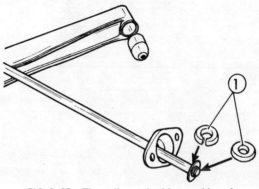

FIG 8:32 The radius rod rubber cushions 1

8:6 Fault diagnosis

(a) Wheel wobble

1 Worn hub bearings
2 Broken or weak front spring
3 Uneven tyre wear
4 Worn suspension linkage
5 Loose wheel fixings
6 Loose hub nut
7 Incorrect tracking

(b) Bottoming of suspension

1 Check 2 in (a)
2 Dampers defective
3 Car overloaded

(c) Heavy steering

1 Defective steering swivels
2 Wrong suspension geometry

(d) Excessive tyre wear

1 Check 4 and 6 in (a) and 2 in (c)

(e) Rattles

1 Check 2 in (a) and 1 in (c)
2 Worn bushes or ball joints
3 Damper attachments loose

(f) Excessive rolling

1 Check 2 in (a) and 2 in (b)

CHAPTER 9

REAR SUSPENSION

9:1 Description

The rear suspension consists of semi-elliptical leaf springs 2 controlled by telescopic hydraulic dampers 5, as shown in **FIG 9:1**. The spring eyes and shackle hangers are fitted with rubber bushes 4, the springs being attached to the rear axle by means of U-bolts.

Apart from an occasional check on the security of mounting point bolts and nuts and on wheel hub nut tightness as described in **Chapter 8, Section 8:2**, the bearing adjustment for rear wheels being carried out in a similar manner to that for front wheels.

9:2 Rear wheel bearings

The rear wheel bearings are mounted inside the rear brake drum and hub unit, the removal of which is described in **Chapter 11**. The bearings should be driven out, if they are worn or damaged, then new bearings carefully tapped into place. Keep the bearings square as they are fitted to the bore and use a flat plate across the bearing to ensure that hammer blows will be taken by the outer race only. Never drive a bearing in by tapping on the inner race.

9:3 Suspension and rear axle removal

Loosen the wheel nuts and raise the rear of the car onto floor stands as shown in **FIG 9:2**. Remove the road wheels. Syphon the brake fluid from the brake master cylinder reservoir, then separate the brake hose 1 from the brake line on both sides, as shown in **FIG 9:3**. Disconnect the handbrake cable at the equaliser.

Remove the damper (shock absorber) lower mounting nuts and separate the dampers 1 from the spring plates 2, as shown in **FIG 9:4**. If the damper is to be removed completely, remove the upper mounting nuts shown in **FIG 9:5**. The dampers must be installed with the protector covers 1 forward, as shown in **FIG 9:6**.

Place a jack beneath the rear axle assembly to support it. Remove the spring shackle 1 bolts from the body sides, as shown in **FIG 9:7**. These bolts must be tightened to 4.0 to 4.8kgm (28.9 to 34.7lb ft) when refitted. Remove the front spring bolts from the spring hangers 1 as shown in **FIG 9:8**. Tighten these bolts to the same torque as the shackle bolts when refitting.

Lower the rear axle assembly and remove from beneath the car. The leaf springs can be removed from the axle after detaching the U-bolts.

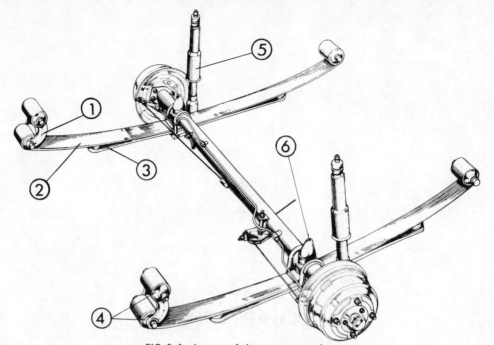

FIG 9:1   Layout of the rear suspension

Key to Fig 9:1   1 Shackle   2 Leaf spring   3 Auxiliary spring   4 Rubber bushes   5 Damper   6 Bump rubber

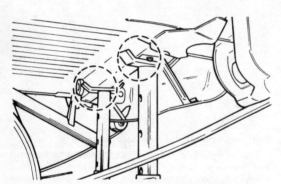

FIG 9:2   Supporting the car at the rear crossmember

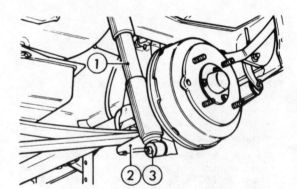

FIG 9:4   Damper 1 lower mounting nut 3

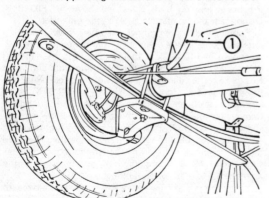

FIG 9:3   Disconnecting the rear brake hoses 1

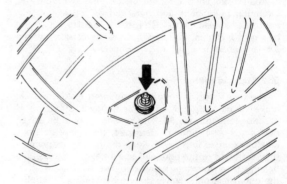

FIG 9:5   Damper upper mounting nuts

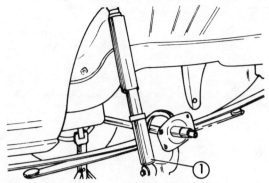

FIG 9:6   Damper protector 1 position

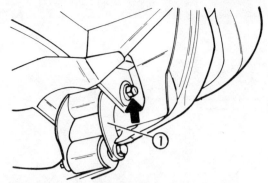

FIG 9:7   The rear spring shackle 1 bolt

When replacement springs are fitted, make sure that the marks on the new springs, as shown in **FIG 9:9**, are installed towards the front of the car.

Refitting:

This is a reversal of the removal procedure. If the car should be lower on one side than the other after refitting the leaf springs, it is due to incorrect fastening of the spring bolts. To correct, loosen the spring bolts on the higher side, have an assistant stand on the body side sill with the door open, then tighten the bolts while the car is thus loaded.

On completion, bleed the brake system and, if necessary, adjust the handbrake cable, all as described in **Chapter 11**.

9:4 Fault diagnosis

(a) Wheel wobble

1 Worn hub bearings
2 Worn spring mounting bushes
3 Uneven tyre wear
4 Loose hub nuts
5 Loose wheel nuts

(b) Bottoming of suspension

1 Broken or weak leaf spring
2 Ineffective dampers
3 Bumper rubbers worn or missing
4 Car overloaded

(c) Rattles

1 Worn bushings
2 Damper attachments loose

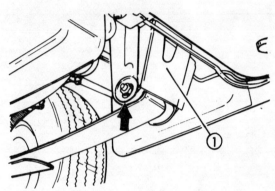

FIG 9:8   The spring hanger 1 bolt

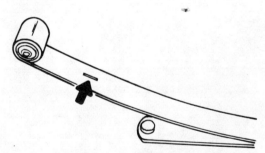

FIG 9:9   The marking on leaf springs to denote the forward end

NOTES

CHAPTER 10

THE STEERING GEAR

10:1 Description

Rack and pinion steering gear is employed on all models, **FIG 10:1** showing the layout of the system. The pinion shaft is turned by the lower end of the universally jointed steering column shaft and moves the rack to the left or right, transmitting the steering motion to the front wheels by means of tie rods and the arms on the steering knuckles. The tie rod ends are connected to the steering knuckles by means of ball joint assemblies, threaded sleeves being provided to allow for front wheel toe-out adjustment. The steering knuckles pivot on the suspension strut assemblies.

10:2 Maintenance

Every 20,000km (12,000 miles) the steering gear should be greased. Grease nipples may be fitted to the rack adjusting bolts, one of which is shown in **FIG 10:3**. If not, an adaptor can be fitted in place of each bolt as shown in **FIG 10:2**. Turn the steering to the extreme left when greasing the lefthand nipple, to the right when greasing the righthand. Apply only three or four strokes of the grease gun, do not over-grease. If an adaptor is used, remove it, refit the adjusting bolt, then check the adjustment as described next.

If the steering gear has excessive play, adjustments may be made at the points shown in **FIG 10:3**. If excessive axial play exists at the pinion, loosen the pinion gear locknut 1 and tighten the mounting bolt 3 a little at a time until play is just eliminated. Tighten the locknut when completed. If there is excessive play in the rotational direction, loosen the locknuts 1 and adjust the bolts 2 at each end of the rack until play is just eliminated. Tighten the locknuts when completed. Check that the force needed to turn the steering wheel when the front wheels are raised clear of the ground does not exceed 1.5kg (3.3lb), using a spring scale as described in **Section 10:4**.

10:3 Steering column and wheel

Removal:

Loosen the clamp bolt 2 at the steering column shaft 1 and pinion gear connection 3, as shown in **FIG 10:4**. Disconnect the electrical wiring 1 and remove the four bolts retaining the steering column to the instrument panel, as shown in **FIG 10:5**. Remove the three retaining screws and remove the crash pad from the centre of the steering wheel.

Remove the screw to disconnect the horn wire from the steering wheel hub, then remove the steering wheel retaining nut. Remove the two screws shown in **FIG 10:6** and separate the horn switch contact plate. Use a puller

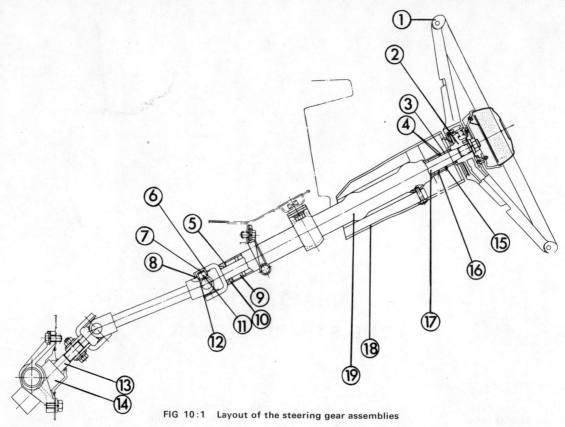

FIG 10:1   Layout of the steering gear assemblies

Key to Fig 10:1   1 Steering wheel   2 Combination switch assembly   3 Cancelling cam   4 Cancelling cam washers   5 Spring   6 Bearing   7 Spring   8 Lockplate   9 Lower bush   10 Rubber ring   11 Cross shaft   12 'O' ring   13 Pinion   14 Steering rack assembly   15 Cancelling cam spring   16 Upper bush   17 Steering shaft   18 Cover   19 Column housing

as shown in **FIG 10:7** to remove the steering wheel from the column shaft. Remove the turn signal cam components as shown in **FIG 10:8**. Take out the single screw and remove the steering column cover.

Loosen the screw shown in **FIG 10:9** completely, then tap the top of the screw with the screwdriver to separate the combination switch from the steering column housing. Use a screwdriver as shown in **FIG 10:10** to remove the lockplates 1, then dismantle the steering shaft universal joints.

Inspection:

Check the steering column top bushing shown in **FIG 10:11** for wear or damage and renew the bushing if necessary.

Check the universal joints for play in both directions. Either a standard joint of the type shown in **FIG 10:12** will be fitted, or the non-serviceable factory sealed type shown in **FIG 10:13**. Excessive play in a standard type joint can be cured by checking the trunnion caps 2 (see **FIG 10:12**) and lockplates 3 for wear and renewing those

FIG 10:2   Greasing adaptor fitted temporarily in place of rack adjusting bolt

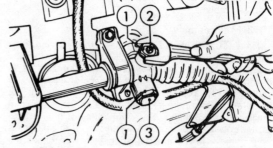

FIG 10:3   Steering gear adjustment points

Key to Fig 10:3   1 Locknuts   2 Rack adjusting bolt   3 Mounting bolt

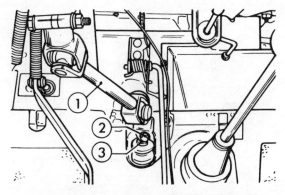

FIG 10:4   Steering shaft 1 to pinion 3, clamp bolt 2

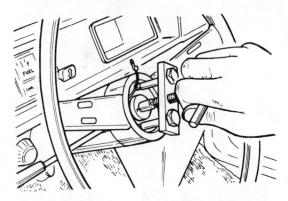

FIG 10:7   Steering wheel removal

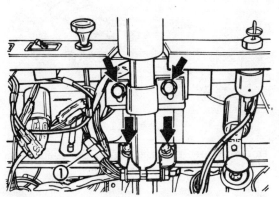

FIG 10:5   Disconnecting the wiring 1 and detaching the steering column

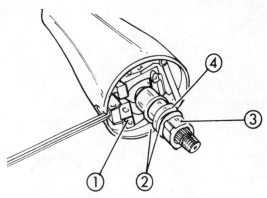

FIG 10:8   Turn signal cam components

Key to Fig 10:8
2 Cancelling cam washers
4 Cancelling cam spring
1 Combination switch assembly
3 Turn signal cancelling cam

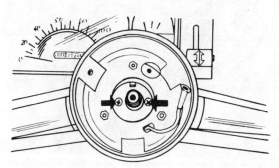

FIG 10:6   Removing the horn switch contact plate

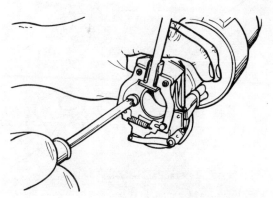

FIG 10:9   Removing the combination switch

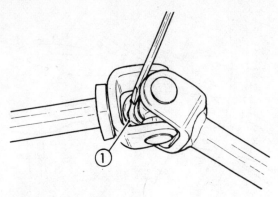

FIG 10:10 Removing the universal joint lockplates 1

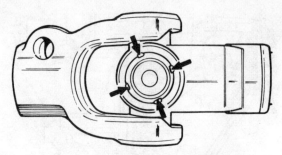

FIG 10:13 Factory sealed universal joint assembly

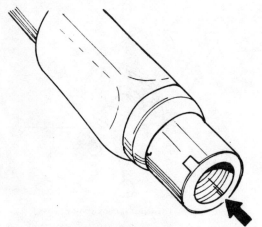

FIG 10:11 The steering column top bushing

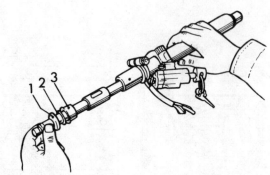

FIG 10:14 Lower bushing 3, spring 2 and cushion rubber 1 installation

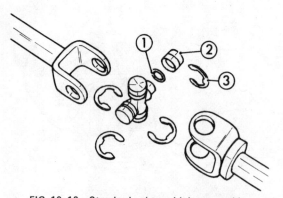

FIG 10:12 Standard universal joint assembly

Key to Fig 10:12   1 'O' ring   2 Trunnion cap
3 Lockplate

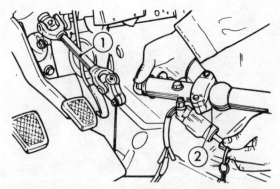

FIG 10:15 Column reassembly on models fitted with a steering lock 2

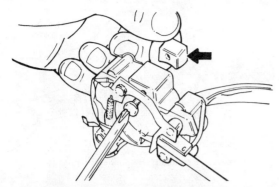

FIG 10:16   The combination switch locking piece

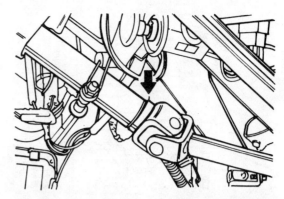

FIG 10:17   Fitting the column housing to the steering shaft

parts found to be defective. Excessive play in a factory-sealed type joint can be cured in most instances by making four punch marks around the inner edge of the yoke, as shown in **FIG 10:13**. If this operation does not cure the play, the joint assembly must be renewed complete. If, after overhaul, a universal joint is stiff to operate, tap the yokes gently with a soft-faced hammer to relieve internal stress.

Installation:

This is a reversal of the removal instructions, noting the following points:

Install the steering shaft with the longer serrated yoke towards the steering gear. Fit the column cushion rubber 1 and spring 2 as shown in **FIG 10:14**, with the flat side of the rubber upward. Renew this cushion rubber if it is at all worn. Models for certain export markets are fitted with steering column locks and on these models the column must be properly aligned. To do this, set the front wheels in the straightahead position, remove the key from the lock and connect the column assembly to the steering shaft, then mount the column assembly loosely in position until all parts have been refitted (see **FIG 10:15**).

Align both grooves of the combination switch and steering column housing when fitting the switch. The tapered locking piece for the switch must be fitted with the circular side towards the housing and the tapered side towards the switch, as shown in **FIG 10:16**.

Prior to installing the turn signal cancelling cam, ensure that the turn signal switch is in the neutral position, to prevent damage to the switch when the steering wheel is fitted. Apply a thin smear of grease to the cam.

Make sure that the front wheels are in the straight-ahead position when fitting the steering wheel, and that the steering wheel spokes are centralised. Tighten the steering wheel retaining nut to 3.0 to 3.5kgm (22 to 25lb ft).

Before tightening the steering column mounting bolts, position the column housing in the proper position and eliminate the play between the steering shaft and the housing, as shown in **FIG 10:17**. Do not make this fit too tight, however, or the cushion rubber may be compressed. Position the column housing so that a clearance of 1 to 4mm (0.04 to 0.16in) exists between the cover and the steering wheel, as shown in **FIG 10:18**.

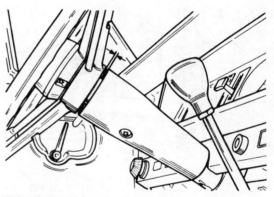

FIG 10:18   Adjusting the clearance between the cover and steering wheel

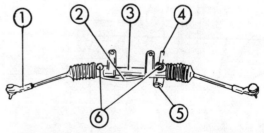

FIG 10:19   Steering gear and tie rod assembly

Key to Fig 10:19   1 Tie rod end and ball joint   2 Breather tube   3 Rack housing   4 Pinion   5 Pinion adjusting bolt   6 Rack adjusting bolt

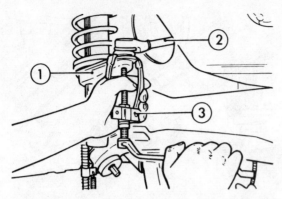

FIG 10:20   Disconnecting the tie rod ball joints

Key to Fig 10:20   1 Knuckle arm   2 Tie rod   3 Ball joint puller

FIG 10:21   The steering gear bolts in the engine compartment

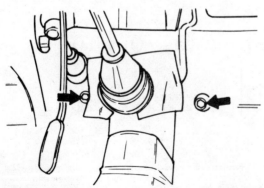

FIG 10:22   The steering gear bolts in the passenger compartment

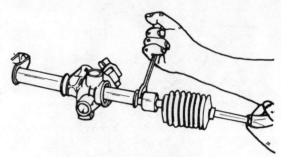

FIG 10:23   Removing the rack end from the rack

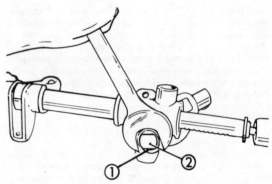

FIG 10:24   Removing the rack and pinion mesh adjusting bolt 2 and locknut 1

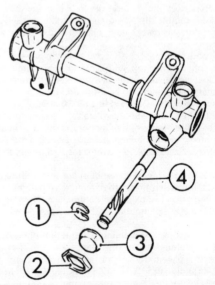

FIG 10:25   Removing the pinion gear assembly

Key to Fig 10:25   1 Thrust plate   2 Locknut   3 Adjusting plug   4 Pinion

10:4 Steering gear

The rack and pinion steering gear and the tie rod assemblies are shown in **FIG 10:19**.

Removal:

Disconnect the tie rods 2 from the steering knuckles 1, using a ball joint puller 3 or similar as shown in **FIG 10:20**. Detach the steering column assembly from the instrument panel and disconnect the steering shaft from the pinion gear as described in **Section 10:3**. Remove the four bolts shown in **FIGS 10:21** and **10:22** and remove the steering gear from the car.

Dismantling:

Unlock the washer and remove the rack end from the rack as shown in **FIG 10:23**, then pull the rack out of the housing. Loosen the locknut 1 and remove the pinion and rack adjusting bolt 2 shown in **FIG 10:24**. Remove the pinion thrust plate 1 as shown in **FIG 10:25**, then drive the pinion gear from the housing.

If necessary, loosen the locknuts 2 and remove the tie rod ends 3 as shown in **FIG 10:26**. Count the number of turns taken to remove the tie rod ends so that they can be refitted in their original positions to ease toe-out setting later.

Inspection:

Wash all parts in petrol or other suitable solvent and dry them. Inspect for wear or damage and renew any unserviceable components. If excessive radial play has been found, check both the pinion gear and the bushing for wear. The bushing 1 is press-fitted in the housing with a damper rubber 2 incorporated, as shown in **FIG 10:27**. When renewing the upper pinion gear bushing, always install an oversize cap to hold the new bushing securely.

Check the rack gear bushings for excessive play. If play between the rack and bushing is greater than 0.06mm (0.0024in) the housing assembly should be renewed.

Assembly:

This is a reversal of the dismantling procedure, noting the following points:

Refit the pinion gear assembly into the housing, with the thrust plate round edges facing inwards. Coat the pinion, thrust plate and mounting plate with grease. Tighten the mounting bolt to 2.0 to 2.5kgm (14.5 to 18.1lb ft) and secure with the locknut. Do not overtighten.

Grease the rack and insert it into the housing, meshing it with the pinion. Use a new lockwasher 3 when fitting the tie rods 4 to the rack ends 1, fitting the tongues on the washers into the grooves in the rack, as shown in **FIG 10:28**. Tighten to 3.5 to 4.0kgm (25 to 29lb ft).

Grease the rack guides A and B shown in **FIG 10:29** and install them correctly with the claws towards the front. Do not interchange the rack guides. Check the 'O' rings 2 fitted to the adjusting bolts 3 and renew them if damaged or deteriorated.

Refitting:

This is a reversal of the removal procedure, noting the following points:

Tighten the steering gear mounting bolts to 2.0 to 2.4kgm (14.5 to 17.4lb ft). Adjust rack guide B first,

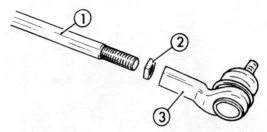

FIG 10:26   Tie rod end removal

Key to Fig 10:26   1 Tie rod   2 Locknut   3 Tie rod end

tightening the adjusting bolt until it stops rotating, then back off about 20°. This is the correct position at which the locknut is tightened. Now adjust rack guide B in the same manner. The locknuts must be tightened to 2.0 to 2.5kgm (14.5 to 18.1lb ft). Do not overtighten.

On completion, check the force needed to turn the steering wheel when the front wheels are raised clear of the ground, jacking up the front of the car and using a spring balance at the wheel rim as shown in **FIG 10:30**. The force needed should not exceed 1.5kg (3.3lb). If this figure is exceeded, check the rack adjustment for overtightness and the steering linkage for binding or stiffness.

Check and adjust the front wheel toe-out setting as described in **Section 10:5**.

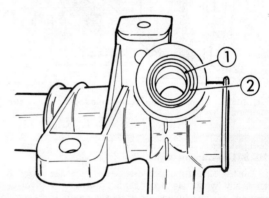

FIG 10:27   The pinion bushing 1 and damper rubber 2

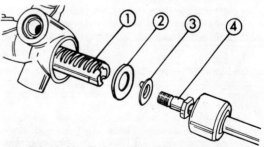

FIG 10:28   Fitting a tie rod to the rack end

Key to Fig 10:28   1 Rack   2 Thrust washer   3 Lockwasher   4 Tie rod

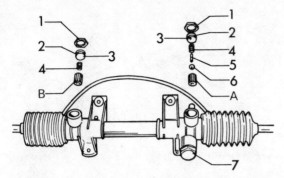

FIG 10:29 Installing the rack guide components

Key to Fig 10:29 1 Locknuts 2 'O' rings 3 Rack adjuster 4 Spring 5 Inner spring 6 Rack guide centre 7 Pinion bolt A Rack guide A B Rack guide B

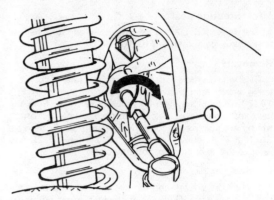

FIG 10:31 Adjustment of the tie rod 1 ends

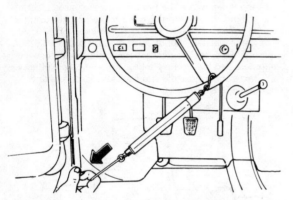

FIG 10:30 Checking the force needed to turn the steering wheel

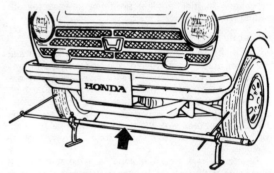

FIG 10:32 Measuring the front wheel toe-out

10:5 Toe-out setting

The toe-out setting of the front wheels must be checked after any work has been carried out which involves removal of the steering gear, loosening of the tie rod locknuts or the disconnecting of tie rod end ball joints. The setting should also be checked if uneven or abnormal tyre wear has been noted.

In order that the checks and adjustments be effective, the steering linkage must be in good condition, with no slack in the ball joints and the wheel bearings must be correctly adjusted as described in **Chapter 8**.

The front wheels must be set so that, in the straight-ahead position, they toe-out 2mm (0.08in). This means that the front of the wheels are pointed away from the car centre line by half the stated amount each, the figure given being the total for both wheels.

The wheel positions are adjusted by locating the tie rod end locknuts and screwing the tie rods 1 in or out of the tie rod ends, as shown in **FIG 10:31**. The adjustment must be carried out equally on each side.

To check the setting, the distance between the front of the wheels must be measured, then the distance between the back of the wheels. Raise the front of the car until the wheels are off the ground, then spin each wheel slowly while holding a sharpened piece of chalk steadily against the centre of the tyre tread. This will mark a reference line around the tyre circumference. Lower the car and push it forward a little to settle the wheels in the straightahead position.

Now measure the distance between the chalk marks on the front tyres, using a gauge or other suitable means, as shown in **FIG 10:32**. Note the figure measured, then roll the car forward until the wheels have turned through 180° (half-a-turn). Now measure between the chalk marks at the rear of the front wheels. The measurement taken at the rear of the wheels should be less than that taken at the front of the wheels by the stated amount. Measurements must be taken at hub centre height. If the correct figure is not obtained, adjustment is necessary.

In order that the toe-out setting is carried out accurately, the owner may prefer to have the work carried out at a service station having special optical track setting equipment, the work taking only a short time when such equipment is to hand.

10:6 Fault diagnosis

(a) Wheel wobble

1 Unbalanced wheels and tyres
2 Slack steering connections
3 Incorrect steering goemetry
4 Excessive play in steering gear
5 Faulty suspension
6 Worn hub bearings

(b) Heavy steering

1 Check 3 in (a)
2 Very low tyre pressures
3 Neglected lubrication
4 Rack too tight
5 Steering column defective

(c) Wander

1 Check 2, 3 and 4 in (a)
2 Uneven tyre pressures
3 Uneven tyre wear
4 Ineffective dampers

(d) Lost motion

1 Loose steering wheel, worn splines
2 Worn rack and pinion teeth
3 Worn ball joints
4 Worn pinion bearings

NOTES

CHAPTER 11

THE BRAKING SYSTEM

11 : 1 Description

The braking system follows conventional practice, with hydraulically operated brake units on all four wheels, the cable operated handbrake linkage operating the rear brake units only.

According to model type and time of manufacture, either leading/trailing shoe or twin leading shoe type front drum brake units may be fitted, leading/trailing shoe drum brakes being fitted to the rear wheels on all vehicles. Front disc brakes are fitted to certain 600 models.

All 360 models and some 600 models with all-drum braking systems are fitted with single master cylinder units, in which one piston supplies brake fluid pressure for both front and rear brakes. On all 600 models equipped with disc brakes and on some 600 models equipped with all-drum systems, dual master cylinder assemblies are provided, in which the fluid circuits for front and rear brakes are separated. This feature ensures that, if either the front or the rear circuit should fail, the car can be safely brought to a halt with the remaining system. If either of the systems in a dual master cylinder assembly should fail, the reduced braking power will be noticed and repairs to the braking system should be carried out immediately. The reduced braking power will be less noticeable if the rear brake circuit fails than if the front brake circuit fails, as the front brakes have much greater stopping power than those at the rear, due to forward weight transfer under deceleration.

The master cylinder, which is supplied with brake fluid from the reservoir, is operated by a short pushrod connected to the brake pedal. Fluid pressure is transmitted to the wheel cylinders or disc brake cylinders by means of a series of metal and flexible pipes.

On certain models, a vacuum operated brake servo is fitted, this uses engine vacuum to assist the effort applied at the brake pedal, the operation and maintenance of this unit being described in **Section 11 : 7**.

11 : 2 Maintenance

Regularly check the level 1 of the fluid in the master cylinder reservoir 2, shown in **FIG 11 : 1**, and replenish if necessary. Wipe dirt from around the cap before removing it and check that the vent hole in the cap is unobstructed. If frequent topping up is required the system should be checked for leaks, but it should be noted that, with disc brake systems, the fluid level will drop gradually over a period of time, due to the movement of caliper pistons

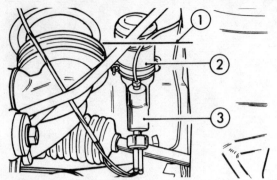

FIG 11:1 Brake master cylinder fluid reservoir
Key to Fig 11:1   1 Fluid level   2 Reservoir   3 Master cylinder

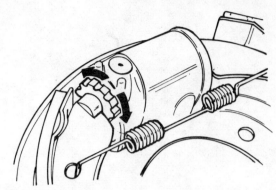

FIG 11:3 Twin leading shoe drum brake adjustment. The brake drum is removed for clarity

compensating for friction pad wear. Use only the correct grade of brake fluid as supplied by a Honda agent. **Never use anything but the correct fluid.**

Checking brake pads and linings:

New disc brake friction pads have a thickness of 10.3mm (0.406in). Check the friction pads on both front wheels at 6000km (3700 mile) intervals. Raise and support the front of the car and remove the road wheels. Examine the friction pads and, if any pad has worn to a thickness of 2.0mm (0.08in) or less, or if any pad is cracked or oily, all four friction pads must be renewed. **Do not renew pads singly or on one side of the car only, as uneven braking will result.**

Check the thicknesses of the brake shoe linings, front and/or rear as appropriate, at the same intervals as front brake friction pads. New linings have a thickness of 5mm (0.197in). Raise and support the car and remove the rear wheels and brake drums, as described later. If any lining is less than 2mm (0.08in) thick at any point, or if any lining is damaged or oily, all four rear brake or front brake linings, whichever is the case, should be renewed.

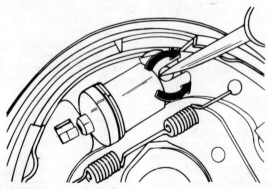

FIG 11:2 Leading/trailing shoe drum brake adjustment. The brake drum is removed for clarity

Brake adjustment:

No adjustments are required for front disc brakes, these being self-adjusting due to the action of the operating pistons in the calipers. These pistons are returned to the rest position after each brake operation by the piston seals, the seals being slightly stretched during brake operation. As the friction pads wear, the piston stroke is increased and the piston will travel further than before and move through the stretched seal a little, the seal returning the piston to a new position nearer to the pads when the brake is released. In this manner the piston stroke remains constant regardless of the thickness of the pads.

All drum brakes should be adjusted whenever brake pedal movement becomes excessive, this operation normally removing any slack in the handbrake linkage at the same time.

Drum brakes:

When working on front brakes, fully apply the handbrake. When working on rear brakes, chock the front wheels and fully release the handbrake.

Raise and safely support the front or rear of the car as appropriate.

On leading/trailing shoe units, turn the road wheel until the adjusting screw shown in **FIG 11:2** can be reached with a screwdriver. Turn the adjusting screw clockwise until the wheel is locked against rotation, then back off the screw just enough to allow the wheel to rotate freely. Press the brake pedal several times to settle the shoes, then recheck the adjustment.

Some models have an alternative type of adjuster which protrudes from the backplate. After removing the rubber dust cap, the squared end of the adjuster can be turned with a spanner and adjustment carried out as described previously.

On twin leading shoe units, turn the road wheel until one of the adjusting star wheels can be reached with a screwdriver, as shown in **FIG 11:3**. Use the tip of the screwdriver to turn the star wheel anticlockwise until the road wheel is locked against rotation, then release the star wheel until the road wheel is just free to turn. This will adjust one of the two brake shoes only, so the operation must be carried out again at the second wheel

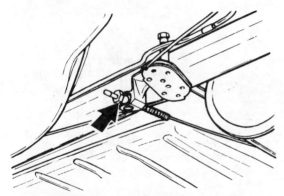

FIG 11:4   The handbrake cable adjuster

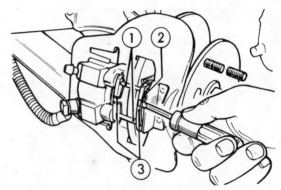

FIG 11:5   Removing the pin retaining clips

Key to Fig 11:5   1 Retaining pins   2 Retaining clip
3 Retaining spring

cylinder on the opposite side of the same brake unit. Both shoes must be equally adjusted at each brake unit. Press the brake pedal several times to settle the shoes, then recheck the adjustment.

Handbrake:

The rear brake shoe adjustment just described will normally take up any slack in the handbrake cable and must always be carried out before any check on hand-brake adjustment is made. If the handbrake cables have been refitted after a service operation or if the cables are stretched, adjust in the following manner:

Pull the handbrake lever on until the ratchet engages with the second or third notch from the fully released position. Raise the rear of the car and safely support on floor stands. At this setting, both rear wheels should be locked against rotation by hand. If not, act on the cable adjuster beneath the car to tighten the brake cable, as shown in **FIG 11:4**. Tighten the cable a little at a time, with the handbrake set as described, turning the rear wheels after each adjustment to check the point at which they are locked against rotation. When this point is reached, lock the adjusting nut, release the handbrake and check for free rotation of the rear wheels. Slacken the cable a little if the wheels are not free to turn. Lubricate the cable with grease at the point where it passes through the adjuster mechanism, so that it slides freely through the adjuster and provides equal force to each brake unit.

11:3   Disc brakes

Disc brake pad renewal:

Raise the front of the car, support safely on floor stands, then remove the road wheels. Remove the pin retaining clip 3 as shown in **FIG 11:5**, then remove the retaining pins 2 and springs 1 as shown in **FIG 11:6**, taking care to prevent the springs from flying out.

The brake pads 1 can now be removed from the caliper, together with the pad shims as shown in **FIG 11:7**. If the pads are difficult to remove, open the bleed screw and move the yoke in the direction of the piston, then close the bleed screw. This will loosen the pads. Do not touch the brake pedal when the pads are removed.

Before fitting the new pads, push the caliper pistons to the bottom of their bore by loosening the bleed screw and applying pressure to the piston face. When the inner

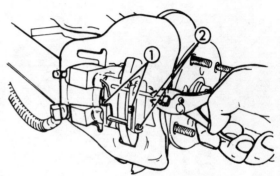

FIG 11:6   Removing the retaining pins 2 and springs 1

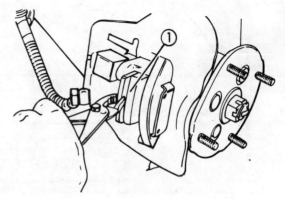

FIG 11:7   Removing the pads 1 and shims

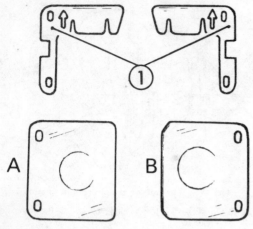

FIG 11:8   Brake pads and shims 1

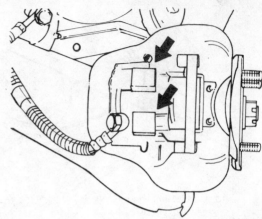

FIG 11:11   Locations of the caliper mounting bolts behind the cylinder

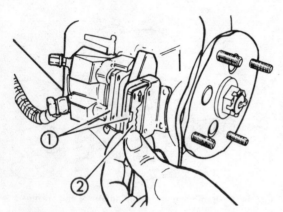

FIG 11:9   Correct installation of pad shims 2

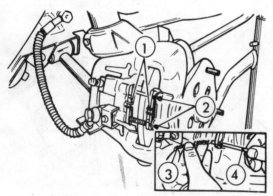

FIG 11:10   Fitting the coil spring 3 to the leading retaining pin 4

piston is butted against the boot retaining ring, tighten the bleed screw. Operating the bleed screw in this way will prevent fluid overflow in the reservoir when the pistons are pushed back. Clean all dirt and dust from the caliper before fitting the new pads, using a suitable brush or a compressed air nozzle.

Install the new pads with the shims 1, noting that the inner B and outer A pads differ slightly, as shown in **FIG 11:8**. The shims 2 are interchangeable with each other, but must be installed with the arrow marks pointing upwards, as shown in **FIG 11:9**. Incorrect shim installation can cause brake squeal.

First install one of the retaining pins 2 then hook one end of the pad retaining spring 1 on this pin. Clip the centre loop over the top of the pad and hold down the opposite end of the spring while pushing the pin through to align with the inside pad and mounting hole. Insert the pin retaining clip into the hole under the head of the pin. The coil spring 3, used to assist full pad release, should be fitted to the leading pin 4 as shown in **FIG 11:10**.

Before using the car on the road, pump the brake pedal several times to adjust the pads to the correct position near the discs. If this is not done, the brakes may not work first time that they are applied.

Servicing a caliper:

Removal:

Remove the friction pads as described previously. Using a universally-jointed socket wrench, remove the two 10mm caliper mounting bolts, the locations of these bolts being indicated in **FIG 11:11**. Hold the caliper assembly and disconnect the flexible brake hose. Note that two shims are fitted between the caliper and the steering knuckle at the mounting points. Take care not to lose these shims.

Dismantling:

FIG 11:12 shows the components of the disc brake caliper. Clean the exterior of the caliper thoroughly to prevent dirt from contaminating the interior components. Tap the cylinder body lightly with a plastic hammer, at the points shown in **FIG 11:13**, to remove the cylinder

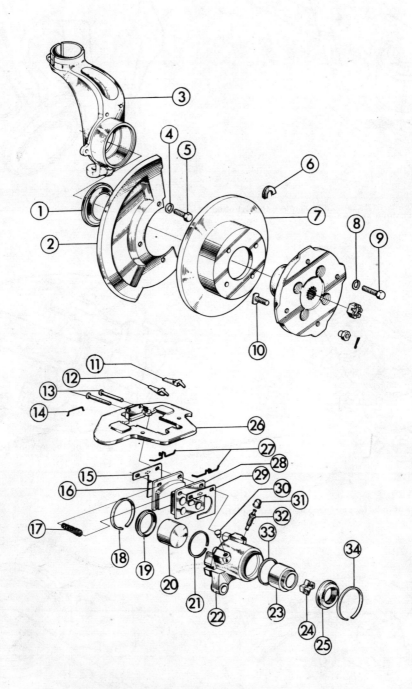

FIG 11:12 Disc brake caliper components

Key to Fig 11:12   1 Seal   2 Splash guard   3 Knuckle   4 Spring washer   5 Bolt   6 Spacer   7 Disc   8 Spring washer
9 Bolt   10 Bolt   11 Yoke spring A   12 Yoke spring B   13 Pins   14 Clip   15 Shim   16 Pad   17 Spring   18 Clip
19 Boot   20 Piston   21 Seal   22 Cylinder   23 Piston   24 Bias ring   25 Boot   26 Yoke   27 Spring   28 Pad
29 Shim   30 Dust plug   31 Cover   32 Bleed screw   33 Seal   34 Clip

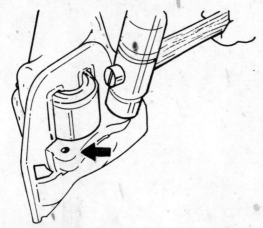

FIG 11:13 Points to be tapped to remove the cylinder body from the caliper assembly

FIG 11:16 Removing the retaining rings and boots

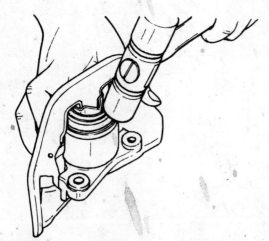

FIG 11:14 Point to be tapped to loosen the outer piston

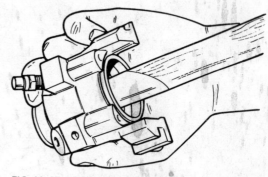

FIG 11:17 Removing the pistons from the cylinder

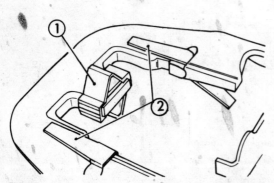

FIG 11:15 Removing the bias ring 1 and yoke springs 2

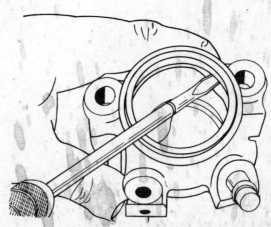

FIG 11:18 Piston seal removal

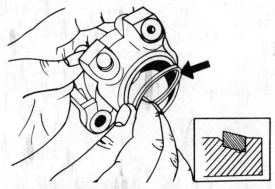

FIG 11:19 Fitting the piston seals to the cylinder bore grooves

body from the caliper assembly. If only the cylinder body moves while the outer piston remains held to the caliper, tap the piston gently. Do not tap the rubber boot at all or it may be damaged. **FIG 11:14** shows the point at which to tap the piston.

Remove the bias ring 1 and the two yoke springs 2 from the caliper, as shown in **FIG 11:15**. Remove the piston boot retaining rings and the boots from both ends of the cylinder as shown in **FIG 11:16**, taking care not to damage the boots. Push both the inner and outer pistons from the cylinder, using a wooden rod as shown in **FIG 11:17**. Remove the piston seals from the cylinder bore as shown in **FIG 11:18**, taking care not to damage the bore surface or the seal groove edges.

Inspection:

Thoroughly clean all internal parts in methylated spirits or clean brake fluid only. Never use any other cleaning agent. Inspect all parts for wear or damage and the pistons and cylinder bore surfaces for scoring or rust marks. Renew all faulty components. Always fit new rubber seals and new bias rings.

Assembly:

This is a reversal of the dismantling procedure. Dip all internal parts in clean brake fluid and assemble them wet. Observe absolute cleanliness during assembly to prevent contamination by dirt, grease or oil. Use the fingers only to fit the new rubber seals, to prevent damage. The seals must be fitted to the cylinder grooves as shown in **FIG 11:19**, making certain that they are the correct way round as shown in the detail.

Apply a thin coat of grease to the sliding surfaces of the caliper and cylinder body, but take care not to get grease near the cylinder or pistons. Align the bias ring in the outer piston so that the slot in the ring fits the cylinder support tongue on the caliper.

Tighten the caliper mounting bolts to 5 to 6kgm (37 to 44lb ft), making sure that the shims are correctly fitted, as shown in **FIG 11:20**. On completion, bleed the brakes as described in **Section 11:6**.

Brake disc removal:

Remove the caliper assembly from the steering knuckle as described previously, but do not disconnect

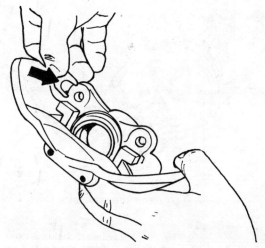

FIG 11:20 Fitting the shims at the caliper mountings

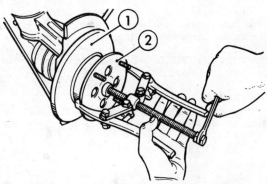

FIG 11:21 Brake disc 1 and hub 2 removal

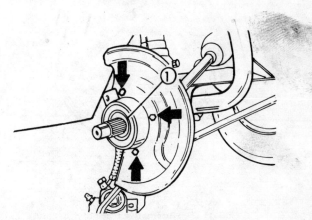

FIG 11:22 Splash shield removal

Key to Fig 11:22 1 Dust seal

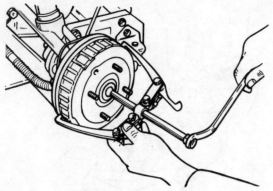

FIG 11 : 23   Brake drum removal

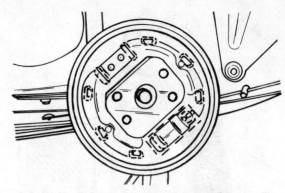

FIG 11 : 25   Points to be greased on leading/trailing shoe brake units

the flexible brake hose. Wire the caliper to the suspension so that the hose is not strained. Remove the cotter pin and wheel spindle nut, then extract the hub 2 and disc assembly 1 as shown in **FIG 11 : 21**, using a suitable puller tool. If necessary, remove the splash shield by removing the bolts shown in **FIG 11 : 22**. Remove the mounting bolts to separate the brake disc from the hub.

Check the condition of the working surfaces of the disc. Slight scoring is unimportant, but deep scoring will accelerate brake pad wear and impair braking performance. Scored discs can be reground at a service station, but thickness must not be reduced to less than 7.6mm (0.299in).

Refitting:

This is a reversal of the removal procedure. Check the front wheel bearing and tighten the hub nut in the manner described in **Chapter 8**, **Section 8 : 2**. As the flexible brake hose has not been disconnected, there should be no need for brake system bleeding.

11 : 4   Drum brakes

Brake shoe renewal:

Before raising the car, remove the hub cap and loosen the wheel nuts, then remove the cotter pin and loosen the wheel hub nut. Raise the car and support safely on floor stands, then remove the road wheel and the hub nut.

Remove the brake drum from the spindle, using a puller as shown in **FIG 11 : 23**. Alternatively, a puller with legs which bolt to the wheel studs may be used.

The brake shoes are mounted in the manner shown in **FIG 11 : 24**, the unit on the left of the illustration showing a leading/trailing shoe type, the unit on the right showing

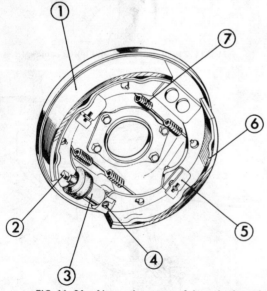

FIG 11 : 24   Alternative types of drum brake unit. Left, leading/trailing type; right, two leading type

Key to Fig 11 : 24   1 Leading shoe   2 Handbrake arm   3 Cylinder   4 Adjusting screw   5 Spring   6 Trailing shoe   7 Return spring   8 Adjuster   9 Cylinder   10 Adjuster   11 Cylinder

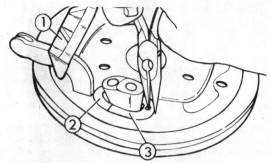

FIG 11:26 Removing the wheel cylinder from leading/trailing shoe brakes

Key to Fig 11:26   1 Dust seal   2 Pressure spring   3 Clip plate

a twin leading shoe type. The shoes are released by unhooking the return springs 7 and twisting and releasing the clamp springs 5.

Slacken the brake adjusters fully, then fit the brake shoes in the reverse order of removal. Apply a thin smear of grease to the points shown in FIG 11:25 for leading/trailing shoe units, noting that the wheel cylinder on this type of brake must slide smoothly. Grease only the shoe web support points on twin leading shoe units. Apply grease sparingly in all cases and take care not to contaminate the shoe linings. Check the inside diameter of the brake drum for good condition. If the working surface is more than 0.1mm (0.004in) out of round or is scored or damaged, regrinding should be carried out at a service station, up to a maximum oversize of 0.5mm (0.02in). Tighten the wheel bearings as described in **Chapter 8, Section 8:2** and adjust the brake shoes as described in **Section 11:2**.

Servicing a wheel cylinder:

On leading/trailing types, remove the brake shoes as described previously. Remove the flexible hose from the wheel cylinder and plug the end of the hose to prevent fluid loss. Disconnect the parking brake cable from the brake arm, if working on a rear brake unit. Remove the brake backplate from the rear axle or steering knuckle. Remove the dust seal 1 and take out the clip plate 3 as shown in FIG 11:26, then remove the pressure spring 2 to release the wheel cylinder. Remove the parking brake arm from the cylinder, if fitted.

On twin leading shoe types, remove the brake shoes as described previously. Remove the flexible hose 2 from the backplate and plug the hose to prevent fluid loss. Remove the backplate, then remove the bridge line 1 and wheel cylinder nuts arrowed and separate the wheel cylinders, as shown in FIG 11:27.

Servicing:

Dismantle the cylinder used with leading/trailing shoe brakes into the order shown in FIG 11:28. On cylinders used with twin leading shoe brakes, remove the adjuster lock spring 1 as shown in FIG 11:29, then dismantle the units into the order shown in FIG 11:30, keeping the parts for each unit together.

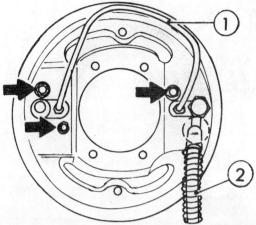

FIG 11:27 Removing the wheel cylinders from twin leading shoe brakes

Key to Fig 11:27   1 Bridge line   2 Brake hose

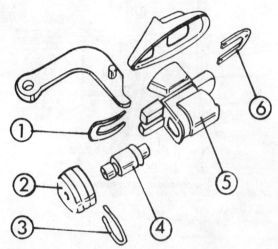

FIG 11:28 Leading/trailing shoe brake wheel cylinder components

Key to Fig 11:28   1 Pressure spring   2 Boot   3 Clip   4 Piston   5 Body   6 Clip plate

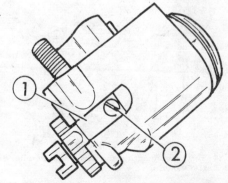

FIG 11:29 Adjuster lock spring 2 on twin leading shoe wheel cylinder

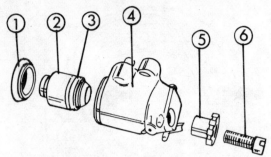

FIG 11:30 Twin leading shoe brake wheel cylinder components

Key to Fig 11:30   1 Boot   2 Piston   3 Piston cup
4 Cylinder body   5 Adjuster   6 Adjuster screw

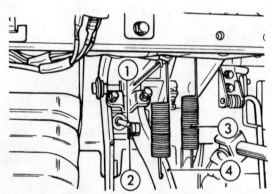

FIG 11:31 Disconnecting the pushrod, single-type or tandem dual-type master cylinder

Key to Fig 11:31   1 Lockpin   2 Link pin   3 Return spring   4 Brake pedal

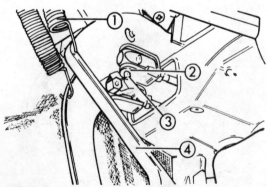

FIG 11:32 Disconnecting the pushrods, parallel dual-type master cylinder

Key to Fig 11:32   1 Return spring   2 Lockpin   3 Linkpin
4 Pedal

Clean all parts in methylated spirits or clean brake fluid and examine them. Check the pistons and cylinder bores for scoring or rust marks and renew them if necessary. Check the diameters of the pistons and the inside diameters of the cylinder bores, using a micrometer and cylinder gauge respectively, then calculate the clearance of each piston in its bore. If this clearance exceeds 0.15mm (0.0059in), the piston, cylinder or both must be renewed as necessary. Always fit new piston cups and rubber boots.

Dip all internal parts in clean brake fluid and assemble them wet, in the reverse order of removal. Refit the wheel cylinders to the backplate, refit the backplate and attach the flexible brake hose, then refit the brake shoes and drum as described previously. On completion, bleed the brakes as described in **Section 11:6**.

11:5 The master cylinder

Removal:

Drain the fluid from the brake system by pumping it out through the bleed screws as described in **Section 11:6**.

On single master cylinder and tandem-type dual master cylinder installations, disconnect the master cylinder pushrod from the brake pedal 4 as shown in **FIG 11:31**, by removing the lockpin 1. On parallel-type dual master cylinder installations, disconnect the master cylinder pushrod by removing the lockpin 2 from the equaliser link, as shown in **FIG 11:32**.

Disconnect the one brake pipe from single master cylinder units. On tandem dual cylinders, disconnect the two reservoir supply tubes and the two brake pipes. On parallel dual cylinders, disconnect the wires from the stop light switches and the two brake pipes. **FIG 11:33** shows the layout of the single master cylinder installation, **FIG 11:34** the installation of a tandem dual master cylinder and **FIG 11:35** the installation of a parallel dual master cylinder. Remove the master cylinder from the car after removing the mounting bolts.

Dismantling and inspection:

Remove the circlip(s) from the end of the master cylinder bore(s) and dismantle the unit into the order shown in **FIG 11:33**, **11:36** or **11:37** as appropriate, **FIG 11:38** showing details of the tandem dual master cylinder piston assembly. On parallel cylinder assemblies, use a piece of wire to remove the check valve seats from position, taking care not to damage the bore surfaces. Note also, on the parallel cylinder unit, that the pushrods are of different lengths, as shown in **FIG 11:39**. If the clevis is removed from any pushrod, its position on the thread should be noted so that it can be refitted in the original position. The equaliser joints 3 are threaded for half their length and must be installed with their threaded sides out. The front pushrod must be installed on the side of the equaliser marked with an F2 and the joint tightened so that one thread projects (see **FIG 11:40**).

Clean all internal parts in methylated spirits or clean brake fluid. Use a compressed air nozzle to clear the fluid inlet and compensating ports in the cylinder casting. Inspect all parts for wear or damage and the piston and cylinder assemblies for scoring or rust marks. Renew any faulty part. Always fit new rubber piston cups.

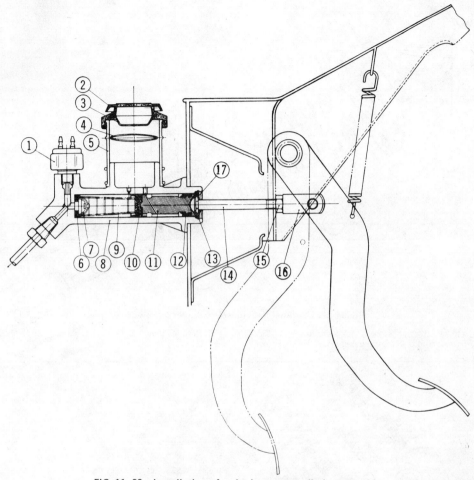

FIG 11:33   Installation of a single master cylinder assembly

Key to Fig 11:33   1 Stop switch   2 Reservoir cap   3 Reflector   4 Float   5 Brake fluid reservoir   6 Check valve seat   7 Check valve   8 Cylinder body   9 Return spring   10 Primary cup   11 Piston   12 Secondary cup   13 Circlip   14 Pushrod   15 Locknut   16 Clevis   17 Dust seal

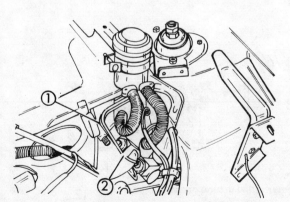

FIG 11:34   Tandem dual master cylinder installation

Key to Fig 11:34   1 Front line   2 Rear line

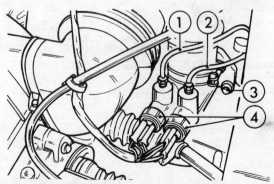

FIG 11:35   Parallel dual master cylinder installation

Key to Fig 11:35   1 Front brake line   2 Rear brake line   3 Mounting bolts   4 Stop switches

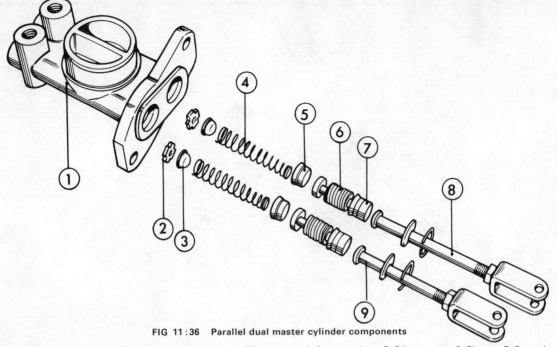

FIG 11:36 Parallel dual master cylinder components

Key to Fig 11:36 1 Cylinder body 2 Valve seat 3 Check valve 4 Return spring 5 Primary cup 6 Piston 7 Secondary cup 8 Front pushrod 9 Rear pushrod

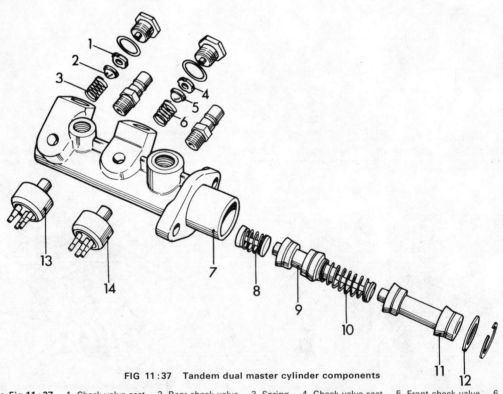

FIG 11:37 Tandem dual master cylinder components

Key to Fig 11:37 1 Check valve seat 2 Rear check valve 3 Spring 4 Check valve seat 5 Front check valve 6 Spring 7 Cylinder body 8 Secondary piston spring 9 Secondary piston 10 Primary piston spring 11 Primary piston 12 Stop ring 13 Rear stop switch 14 Front stop switch

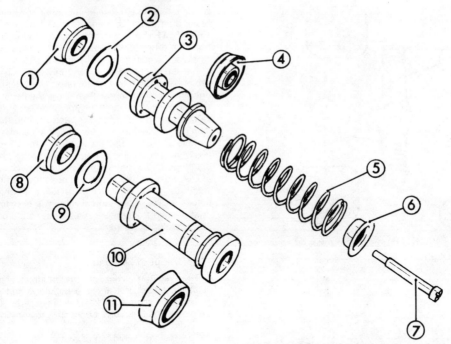

FIG 11:38 Tandem dual master cylinder piston assembly

Key to Fig 11:38   1 Primary cup   2 Wave washer   3 Secondary piston   4 Secondary cup   5 Primary piston spring
6 Secondary piston stop   7 Screw   8 Primary cup   9 Wave washer   10 Primary piston   11 Secondary cup

Use a feeler gauge to check piston to cylinder clearance. If this clearance exceeds 0.15mm (0.0059in), the piston, cylinder or both must be renewed.

Dip all internal parts in clean brake fluid and assemble them wet, in the reverse order of dismantling.

Refitting:

Refit the master cylinder assembly to the car in the reverse order of removal. On completion, bleed the system as described in **Section 11:6**.

11:6 Bleeding the system

This is not routine maintenance and is only necessary if air has entered the system due to parts being dismantled, or because the fluid level has been allowed to drop too low. The need for bleeding is indicated by a spongy feeling of the brake pedal accompanied by poor braking performance. On dual circuit braking systems, this must not be confused with the sharp drop in brake efficiency accompanied by greater pedal travel which indicates failure in one of the circuits. This latter condition must be investigated immediately and the fault rectified.

If, on dual systems, work has been carried out on front brakes only or rear brakes only, then it will normally be necessary to bleed only the circuit (front or rear) that is affected, as the other system should not have been disturbed. If both dual circuits have been disturbed, if any

circuit on single master cylinder systems has been disturbed, or if poor braking performance is evident, bleeding must be carried out at all four wheels. Bleeding must be carried out by starting with the wheel which is furthest from the master cylinder, then by proceeding in order to finish at the wheel nearest to the master cylinder. **Do not bleed the brakes with any drum or caliper removed, or with any brake line disconnected.**

Check the fluid level in the supply reservoir and top up if necessary. Clean around the bleed screws and remove the dust caps. Attach a length of transparent plastic tube to the appropriate bleed screw and lead the free end

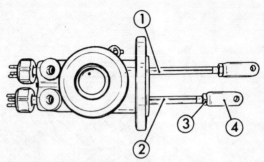

FIG 11:39 Parallel master cylinder pushrods

Key to Fig 11:39   1 Front pushrod   2 Rear pushrod
3 Locknut   4 Clevis

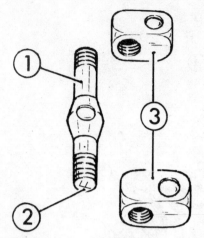

FIG 11:40   Parallel master cylinder pushrod equaliser

Key to Fig 11:40   1 Equaliser   2 F mark   3 Equaliser joints

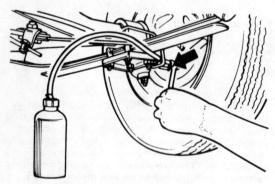

FIG 11:41   Bleeding the brake system

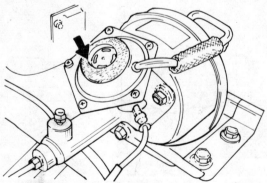

FIG 11:42   Vacuum servo air filter removal

of the tube into a transparent container, adding sufficient brake fluid to the container to cover the end of the tube. **FIG 11:41** shows the bleeding operation being carried out at a drum brake wheel cylinder. Disc brake caliper bleed screw location can be seen in **FIG 11:12**.

Loosen the bleed screw and have an assistant depress the brake pedal firmly to the floor. Hold the pedal down, tighten the bleed screw, then allow the pedal to return to the rest position. Repeat the operation until no air bubbles can be seen passing through the tube into the container, then tighten the bleed screw while the pedal is held down, remove the tube and fit the dust cap. Check the fluid level in the reservoir frequently during the bleeding operation and continue topping up as necessary.

Discard all dirty fluid. If it is perfectly clean, allow it to stand for at least 24hr to ensure freedom from air bubbles before re-use. As a general rule, it is best to discard all fluid drained from the system. Always store brake fluid in clean, sealed containers.

11:7 Vacuum servo unit

The vacuum servo unit is mounted between the master cylinder unit and the bulkhead and operates to assist the pressure applied at the brake pedal. The vacuum cylinder in the servo is connected to the engine intake manifold by a hose.

To test the servo unit, switch off the engine and depress the brake pedal several times to clear all vacuum from the system. Hold a steady light pressure on the brake pedal and start the engine. If the servo is working correctly, the brake pedal should move further downward without further foot pressure, due to the build up of vacuum in the system. If the servo does not operate correctly, check the filter as described next. If a clogged filter is not the cause of the trouble, have the unit checked at a service station. If the servo fails, brake efficiency will be unchanged, but greater pedal pressure will be needed to stop the car.

Servicing:

Every 10,000km (6000 miles), the filter unit in the vacuum servo should be removed and cleaned in methylated spirits. No other cleaning agent should be used.

Remove the valve body cap with a screwdriver and detach the filter unit as shown in **FIG 11:42**. Refitting is a reversal of this procedure.

11:8 Fault diagnosis

(a) Spongy pedal

1 Leak in hydraulic system
2 Worn master cylinder
3 Leaking wheel or caliper cylinders
4 Air in the fluid system

(b) Excessive pedal movement

1 Check 1 and 4 in (a)
2 Excessive lining or pad wear
3 Very low fluid level in supply reservoir
4 Brakes require adjustment

(c) Brakes grab or pull to one side

1 Distorted discs or drums
2 Wet or oily pads or linings
3 Loose backplate or caliper
4 Disc or hub loose
5 Worn suspension or steering connections
6 Mixed linings of different grades
7 Uneven tyre pressures
8 Broken shoe return springs
9 Seized handbrake cable

(d) Brakes partly or fully locked on

1 Swollen pads or linings
2 Damaged brake pipes preventing fluid return
3 Master cylinder compensating hole blocked
4 Master cylinder piston seized
5 Brake shoe return spring broken

6 Dirt in the hydraulic system
7 Seized wheel cylinder or caliper piston

(e) Brake failure

1 Empty fluid reservoir
2 Broken hydraulic pipeline
3 Ruptured master cylinder seal
4 Ruptured wheel cylinder or caliper seal

(f) Reservoir empties too quickly

1 Leaks in pipelines or connections
2 Deteriorated cylinder seals

(g) Pedal yields under continuous pressure

1 Faulty master cylinder seals
2 Faulty wheel cylinder or caliper seals

NOTES

CHAPTER 12

THE ELECTRICAL SYSTEM

12 : 1 Description

All models covered by this manual have 12-volt electrical systems in which the negative terminal of the battery is earthed to the car bodywork.

There are wiring diagrams in **Technical Data** at the end of this manual which will enable those with electrical experience to trace and correct faults.

Instructions for servicing the items of electrical equipment are given in this chapter, but it must be pointed out that it is not sensible to try to repair units which are seriously defective, electrically or mechanically. Such faulty equipment should be replaced by new or reconditioned units.

12 : 2 The battery

To maintain the performance of the battery it is essential to carry out the following operations, particularly in winter when heavy current demands must be met.

Keep the top and surrounding parts of the battery clean and dry, as dampness can cause current leakage. Clean off corrosion from the metal parts of the battery mounting with diluted ammonia and coat them with anti-sulphuric paint. Clean the terminal posts and smear them with petroleum jelly, tightening the terminal clamps securely.

High electrical resistance due to corrosion at the battery terminals can be responsible for a lack of sufficient current to operate the starter motor.

Every three months or 5000km (3000 miles) whichever is the sooner, check the electrolyte level in the battery and, if necessary, add distilled water to the level of the indicator.

If a battery fault is suspected, test the condition of the cells with an hydrometer. **Never add neat acid to the battery. If it is necessary to prepare new electrolyte due to loss or spillage, add sulphuric acid to distilled water. It is highly dangerous to add water to acid.** It is safest to have the battery refilled with electrolyte, if it is necessary, by a service station.

The indications from the hydrometer readings of the electrolyte specific gravity are as follows:

For climates below 27°C or 80°F			Specific gravity
Cell fully charged	..	..	1.270 to 1.290
Cell half discharged	..	..	1.190 to 1.210
Cell discharged	..	..	1.110 to 1.130

For climates above 27°C or 80°F			
Cell fully charged	..	..	1.210 to 1.230
Cell half discharged	..	..	1.130 to 1.150
Cell discharged	..	..	1.050 to 1.070

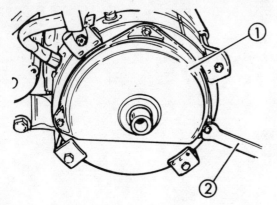

FIG 12:1   Generator cover 1 removal

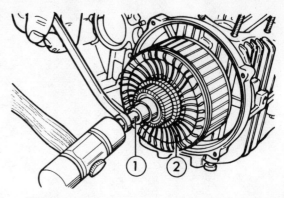

FIG 12:4   Removing the starter/generator rotor 2

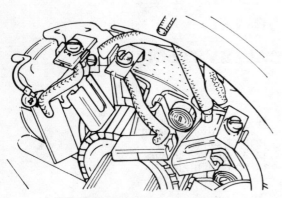

FIG 12:2   Checking the brushes

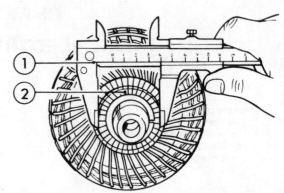

FIG 12:5   Measuring commutator 2 diameter with vernier gauge 1

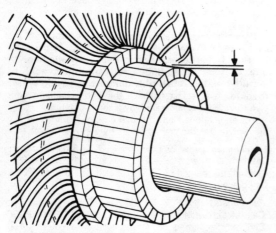

FIG 12:3   Checking insulation undercut depth

FIG 12:6   The crankshaft guide pin

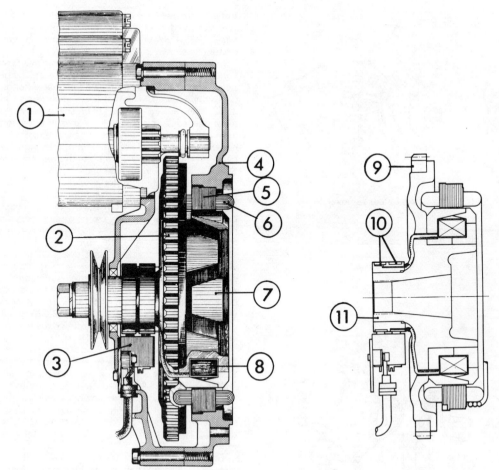

FIG 12:7   Section through the alternator unit

Key to Fig 12:7   1 Starter motor   2 Ring gear   3 Brush holder   4 Flywheel housing   5 Stator core   6 Stator coil   7 Rotor
8 Rotor coil   9 Ring gear   10 Slip rings   11 Rotor

These figures assume an electrolyte temperature of 60°F or 16°C. If the temperature of the electrolyte exceeds this, add 0.002 to the readings for each 5°F or 3°C rise. Subtract 0.002 for any corresponding drop below the figures stated.

All cells should read approximately the same. If one cell differs radically from the others, it may be due to an internal fault or to spillage or leakage of the electrolyte.

If the battery is in a low state of charge, take the car for a long daylight run or put the battery on a charger at 5amps, with the filler caps removed, until it gasses freely. Do not use a naked light near the battery as the gas is inflammable. If the battery is to stand unused for long periods, give a refreshing charge every month. It will be ruined if it is left uncharged.

12:3 The starter motor/generator unit

This unit is installed on 360 models only and is mounted on the end of the crankshaft at the righthand side of the engine (see **FIG 1:3**). The motor/generator operates as a starter and, when the engine is running, as a generator to power the electrical system and charge the battery.

If the starter will not operate or lacks power, or if the charge rate is low, check the condition of the battery and the wiring and connections between the units in the appropriate circuit. If the wiring is in order and the battery in good condition, check the brushes, brush springs and commutator as described later. If, after these items have been checked and serviced, the unit fails to operate correctly, the voltage regulator and the rotor wiring should be checked at an auto-electrical service station having the appropriate test equipment.

Special tools are needed to remove the crankshaft pulley and the starter/generator rotor, although brush and commutator servicing can be carried out with the rotor in position.

Servicing:

Remove the battery from the car. Remove the bolt which retains the crankshaft pulley, then remove the drive belt as described in **Chapter 4**. The pulley has two flat

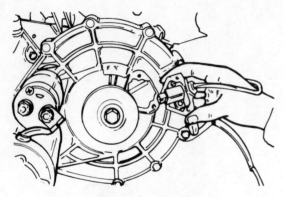

FIG 12:8   Brush holder removal

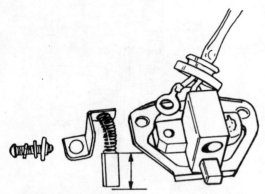

FIG 12:9   Checking the alternator brushes

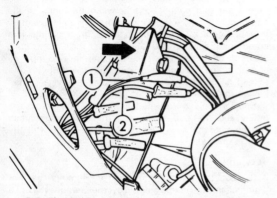

FIG 12:10   Disconnecting the alternator wiring

surfaces inward and the special tool for removal is inserted and forced against these surfaces to grip the pulley. With the pulley removed, remove the generator cover 1 as shown in **FIG 12:1**.

Raise the brush springs and pull the brushes from their holders as shown in **FIG 12:2**. If any brush is worn to a point at or near to the wear limit line marked on its side, renew the brush. Check that each brush slides smoothly in its holder, easing the sides of brushes against a smooth file if they stick or bind. With brushes in good condition installed, check the tension of each brush spring by hooking a spring scale on the end of the spring where it bears on the brush. Any spring with a tension less than 500g (1.1lb) should be renewed.

Check the commutator for condition. If in good condition it will be clean and free from pitting and burned segments. Clean with a cloth and petrol and, if necessary, polish with fine glasspaper. **Do not use emerycloth.** A badly worn commutator must be removed and skimmed in a lathe, taking a light cut with a sharp tool at a high speed. Note that the wear limit must not be exceeded when this work is carried out, or rotor renewal will be necessary. Measure the depth of the undercutting in the mica segments as shown in **FIG 12:3**. This depth must be not less than 0.2mm (0.008in). If less than this, undercut to a depth of 0.5 to 0.8mm (0.020 to 0.032in), using a hacksaw blade ground to the correct width, or a special saw.

If the rotor is to be removed, or to improve access to the commutator, remove the starter and brush gear assembly. Remove the rotor 2 with the special remover tool 1, as shown in **FIG 12:4**. Thread the tool fully into position, tap the tool lightly with a hammer, then pull off the rotor. If the commutator 2 is worn or has been skimmed, check the diameter with calipers 2 as shown in **FIG 12:5**. If the diameter is less than 49mm (1.93in), the rotor must be renewed.

Reassemble the unit in the reverse order of dismantling, aligning the crankshaft guide pin with the rotor, as shown in **FIG 12:6**.

12:4   The alternator

This type of unit is fitted to 600 models, these models using a separate starter motor as described in **Section 12:5**. The alternator provides current for the various items of electrical equipment and to charge the battery, the unit operating at all engine speeds. The current produced is alternate, this being rectified to a direct current supply by diodes connected into the charging circuit. The alternator rotor is mounted on the end of the engine crankshaft (see **FIG 1:4**), a section through the unit being shown in **FIG 12:7**.

If the unit is not charging correctly, check the brushes and renew them if necessary and clean the rotor slip rings, as described later. If more serious faults are evident, the car should be taken to an auto-electrical service station having special checking equipment, for tests to be made.

The alternator must never be run with the battery disconnected, nor must the battery cables be reversed at any time. Test connections must be carefully made, and the battery and alternator wiring must be completely disconnected before any electric welding is carried out on any part of the car. These warnings must be observed, otherwise extensive damage to the alternator components, particularly the diodes, will result.

Checking brushes and slip rings:

Remove the cooling fan belt from the pulley as described in **Chapter 4**. Take out the two set screws and remove the brush holder assembly as shown in **FIG 12:8**. Check the brushes as shown in **FIG 12:9**, renewing if worn to a length of 7mm (0.276in) or less. Use a clean cloth moistened in petrol to clean the rotor slip rings against which the brushes act, working through the brush holder aperture and turning the engine slowly for access to the entire circumference of the rings. Refit the brush holder and fan belt on completion, then check the operation of the units.

Alternator removal:

Disconnect the negative cable from the battery, then refer to **FIG 12:10**. Remove the four white leads from the rectifier arrowed. Separate the white/red striped lead 2 from the black lead 1 connected to the alternator brush at the connector positions.

Remove the starter motor 2 as described later. Remove the cooling fan belt 1 from the crankshaft pulley, as described in **Chapter 4**. Using two spanners as shown in **FIG 12:11**, hold the pulley shaft and remove the pulley retaining bolt, followed by removal of the pulley 3.

Remove the brush holder assembly as described previously. Remove the retaining set bolts (see **FIG 12:8**) and remove the flywheel housing cover.

When removing the rotor, install a holder 1 such as the special tool shown in **FIG 12:12**, installed with two of the housing bolts. Fully thread in the special rotor remover

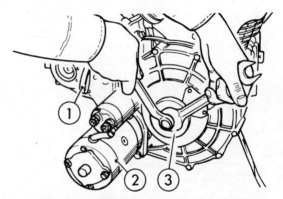

FIG 12:11   Removing the crankshaft pulley 3

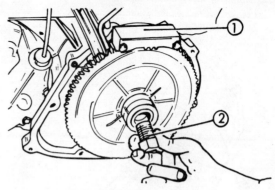

FIG 12:12   Rotor removal

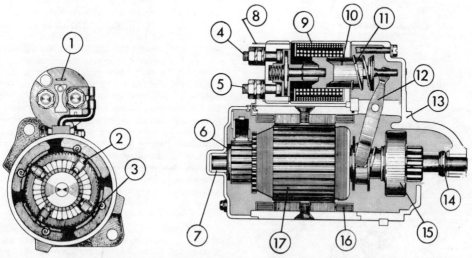

FIG 12:13   Sections through the pre-engaged starter motor

Key to Fig 12:13   1 S terminal   2 Brush   3 Brush spring   4 B terminal   5 M terminal   6 Thrust washer   7 Bush   8 S terminal   9 Solenoid   10 Armature   11 Return spring   12 Lever   13 Casing   14 Stop ring   15 Overrunning clutch   16 Field coil   17 Armature

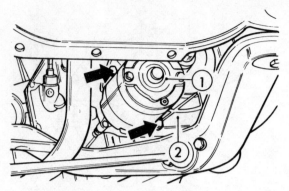

FIG 12:14 Removing the starter motor 1

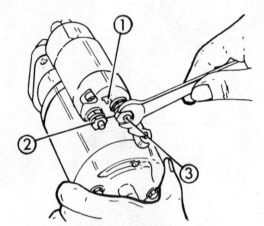

FIG 12:15 Loosening the M terminal nut 3

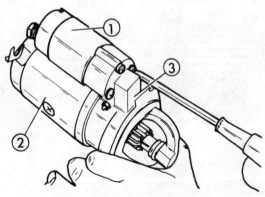

FIG 12:16 Solenoid removal

tool 2 and tap the rotor out while hammering the head of the remover tool lightly. The rotor is a taper fit on the shaft.

Take out the four flywheel housing bolts and remove the housing complete with the stator unit.

Refitting:

This is a reversal of the removal procedure. When installing the flywheel housing cover, make sure that the two hollow pins are correctly fitted. When installing the pulley, align the pulley shaft pawl with the end notch on the crankshaft.

12:5 Pre-engaged type starter

This type of starter motor is fitted to 600 models and used in conjunction with a separate alternator unit as described in **Section 12:4**.

The starter is a brush-type series wound motor equipped with an overrunning clutch and operated by a magnetic switch (solenoid). The armature shaft is supported in special bushes which require no maintenance between overhauls. **FIG 12:13** shows sectional views of the starter motor.

When the starter is operated from the switch, the shift lever 12 moves the pinion into mesh with the ring gear. When the pinion meshes with the ring gear teeth, the solenoid 9 contact disc closes the circuit and the starter motor operates to turn the engine. When the engine starts, the speed of the ring gear causes the pinion to overrun the clutch and armature. The pinion continues in engagement until the shift lever is released, when it returns under spring action.

Tests for a starter which does not operate:

Check that the battery is in good condition and fully charged and that its connections are clean and tight. Switch on the headlamps and operate the starter switch. Current is reaching the starter if the lights dim when the starter is operated, in which case it will be necessary to remove the starter for servicing. If the lights do not dim significantly, switch them off and operate the starter switch while listening for a clicking sound at the starter motor which will indicate that the solenoid is operating.

If no sound can be heard at the starter when the switch is operated, check the wiring and connections between the battery and the starter switch in the passenger compartment and between the switch and the solenoid at the starter motor. If the solenoid can be heard operating when the switch is operated, check the wiring and connections between the battery and the main starter terminals, taking care not to accidentally earth the battery to starter motor lead. If the wiring or connections are not the cause of the trouble, the fault is internal and the starter motor must be removed and serviced.

Removing the starter:

Disconnect the battery negative cable, then remove the splash shield from beneath the car. Remove the main starter cable and the leads from the B(4) and S(8) terminals on the solenoid 9, removing the black lead first followed by the white lead. Remove the two retaining bolts shown in **FIG 12:14**, then remove the starter motor 1 from the flywheel housing cover 2.

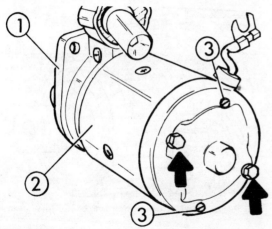

FIG 12:17   Rear cover bolts arrowed and brush holder screws 3

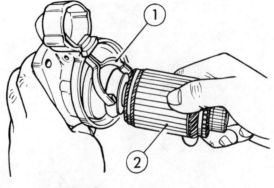

FIG 12:19   Armature 2 removal

Dismantling :

Loosen the M terminal nut 3 shown in **FIG 12:15** and remove the cable. Remove the three screws shown in **FIG 12:16** and remove the solenoid 1 together with the return spring.

FIG 12:17 shows the starter rear cover fixings. The two screws 3 secure the brush holder to the cover, while the two bolts arrowed secure the cover to the yoke 2. Remove these two bolts to separate the cover from the yoke. Remove the four brushes from their holders, then separate the holder from the cover.

Separate the gear case 1 from the starter yoke 4 as shown in **FIG 12:18**, noting that the yoke is provided with a hole into which the yoke lockpin fits. Remove the shift lever pin 2 then remove the plunger 3 from the shift lever. Draw out the armature 2 from the gear case and remove the shift lever 1 as shown in **FIG 12:19**.

FIG 12:20 shows the armature and clutch components. After removing the thrust plate A shown at 1, remove the pinion stop washer 2 by wrenching it out with a screwdriver, as shown in **FIG 12:21**. Slide the pinion stop towards the armature, then remove the stop clip with pliers as shown in **FIG 12:22**. Remove the pinion sleeve clip 5, then dismantle the pinion into the order shown in **FIG 12:23**.

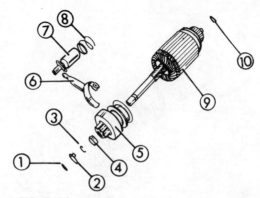

FIG 12:20   Armature and clutch components

Key to Fig 12:20   1 Thrust plate A   2 Pinion stop washer
3 Pinion stop clip   4 Pinion stop   5 Pinion assembly
6 Shift lever   7 Plunger   8 Plunger return spring
9 Armature   10 Thrust plate B, C

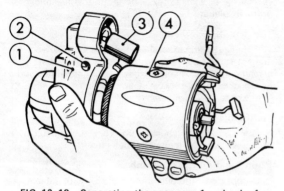

FIG 12:18   Separating the gear case 1 and yoke 4

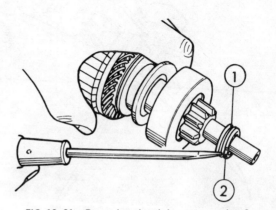

FIG 12:21   Removing the pinion stop washer 2

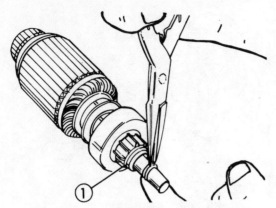

FIG 12:22　Removing the pinion stop clip

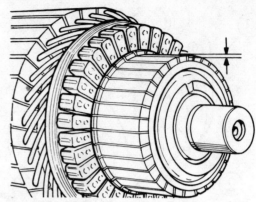

FIG 12:25　Undercutting the commutator insulation

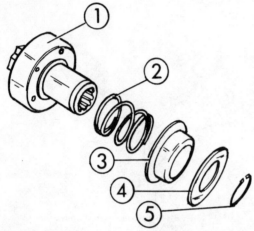

FIG 12:23　Pinion and overrunning clutch components

Key to Fig 12:23　　　　1 Pinion and overrunning clutch
2 Spring　3 Sleeve　4 Washer　5 Circlip

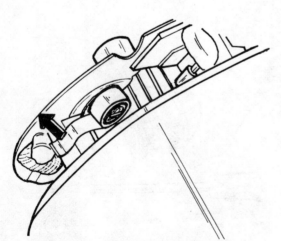

FIG 12:24　Checking brush spring tension

Servicing:

Brush gear:

Check the brushes and renew them if worn to a length of 12.5mm (0.492in) or less. If a brush binds or moves sluggishly in its holder, remove it and ease the sides against a smooth file. Clean the inside of the holder before refitting the brush.

With the brushes fitted, check the tension of the brush springs by pulling up at the point shown in **FIG 12:24** with a spring scale. Renew any spring with a tension less than 0.7kg (1.5lb). If any spring has a tension greater than 0.9kg (1.98lb), adjust to the correct value by bending the spring.

The commutator:

A commutator in good condition will be smooth and free from pitting and burned segments. Clean with a cloth and petrol and, if necessary, polish with fine glasspaper. **Do not use emerycloth.** Skim a badly worn commutator in a lathe, using a high speed and taking a light cut with a sharp tool. Remove the minimum amount necessary to clean up, then polish with fine glasspaper. Note that the wear limit for the commutator is 33mm (1.299in). If the diameter of the commutator is less than this, the armature assembly must be renewed. Undercut the mica between the segments as shown in **FIG 12:25**, to a depth of 0.5 to 0.8mm (0.020 to 0.032in), using a special file or a hacksaw blade ground to the thickness of the insulation.

The armature:

A damaged armature should always be renewed. No attempt should be made to straighten a bent shaft or to machine the core. An electrically suspect armature should be checked by a service station having the necessary armature testing facilities.

Field coils:

These should be checked on proper equipment by a service station and renewed if defective.

Pinion and clutch assembly:

Do not clean the overrunning clutch with solvents as this would wash the internal lubricant from the assembly.

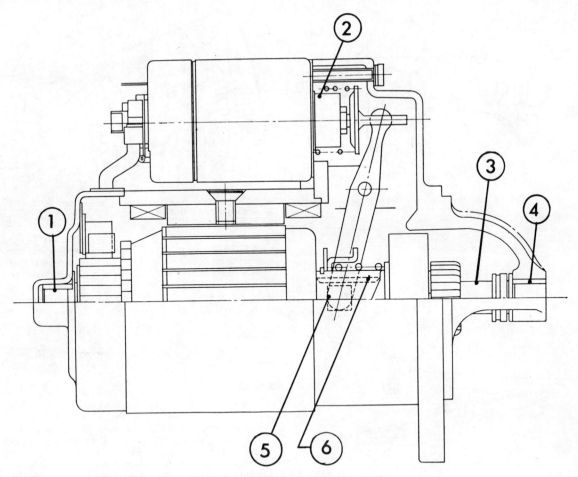

FIG 12:26 Starter motor lubrication points

Key to Fig 12:26 . 1 Rear cover bearing 2 Plunger 3 Pinion shaft 4 Bearing 5 Lever 6 Splines

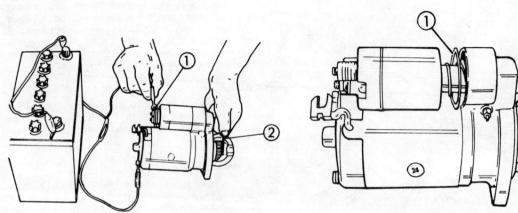

FIG 12:27 Checking pinion engagement mechanism

FIG 12:28 The solenoid adjusting plate 1

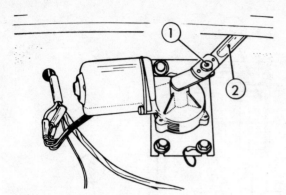

FIG 12:29   Wiper motor installation

Key to Fig 12:29   1 Pin   2 Link

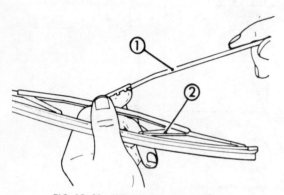

FIG 12:30   Wiper blade 2 installation

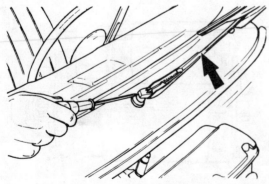

FIG 12:31   Wiper arm removal

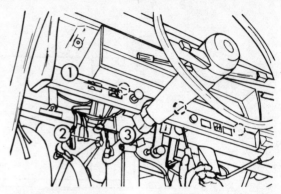

FIG 12:32   Standard instrument panel wiring 2 and mounting screws circled

Check the sliding pinion for smooth operation and the gear teeth for good condition. Check the clutch for proper operation by turning the pinion. The pinion should lock in the drive direction but turn freely in the opposite direction. Renew parts as necessary to correct any fault.

Solenoid:

Check the components of the solenoid and shift lever mechanism, renewing any part found worn or damaged.

Reassembly:

This is a reversal of the dismantling procedure, making sure that the gear case dowel pin is fitted in the hole in the starter yoke. Apply grease sparingly to the points shown in FIG 12:26, taking care not to allow grease to contaminate the brush gear or commutator.

Check the pinion engagement mechanism by connecting the battery to the solenoid connection as shown in FIG 12:27. The starter motor leads are disconnected for this test. Connect the positive (+) lead to the S terminal 1 and the negative (−) lead to the metal part of the solenoid. The pinion will then be moved out by the switch and shift mechanism. Press the pinion gently back to take up play, then measure the gap between the pinion end and the pinion stop, using a feeler gauge 2 as shown. If this clearance is not between 0.3 and 1.5mm (0.012 and 0.059in), the adjusting plate 1 shown in FIG 12:28 must be changed to bring the clearance to within specifications. Adjusting plates can be obtained in 0.4mm and 0.8mm thicknesses.

Refitting:

This is a reversal of the removal procedure, tightening the starter mounting bolts to 3.8 to 4.2kgm (28 to 30lb ft). Make sure that the starter wiring connections are clean and tight.

12:6 Windscreen wipers

The wiper motor installation is shown in FIG 12:29. If the wiper motor is inoperative, check the fuse, wiring and connections. If the motor runs but operation is slow, noisy or laborious, check the linkage for binding or

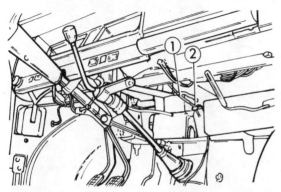

FIG 12:33 Disconnecting the heater control cable 1

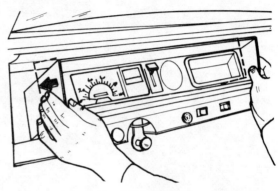

FIG 12:34 Sliding the console outward

damage. The motor operation can be checked by removing the cotter pin 1 shown in **FIG 12:29** and disconnecting the link 2. When switched on, the motor should then run at 45 to 55rev/min. If not, the motor is faulty.

Dismantling of the motor, link and arms should be avoided. If any faults are present, renewal should be carried out, as no repairs are possible.

Wiper blade removal:

Depress the arm link where the blade is connected to the arm, then pull out the blade. Refit by pressing the arm 1 into the link until it locks, as shown in **FIG 12:30**.

Wiper arm removal:

Remove the lockbolt from the end of the wiper arm spindle as shown in **FIG 12:31**, then pull off the arm. When refitting, tighten the lockbolt to 40 to 50kgcm (2.9 to 3.6lb ft).

12:7 Instrument panel

Note that the illustrations shown in this section are for lefthand drive cars, righthand drive car instrument panels being opposite-hand assemblies but otherwise identical.

Instrument removal, standard panel:

Disconnect the battery, then refer to **FIG 12:32**. Disconnect the combination meter wiring connector 2. Disconnect the speedometer cable from behind the panel. Remove the three console mounting screws from the positions shown by broken-line circles. Note that, on some models, the outer screw cannot be removed unless the wiper switch is removed first.

Disconnect the heater control cable 1 at the valve end, as shown in **FIG 12:33**. Slide the console outward about 20mm (0.8in) as shown in **FIG 12:34**, then pull the console from the panel as shown in **FIG 12:35**. In this position, sufficient access is provided for instrument removal. If the console must be completely removed, it must be released from the sliding rail on the instrument panel.

To separate the combination instrument unit from the console, remove the five screws shown in **FIG 12:36**.

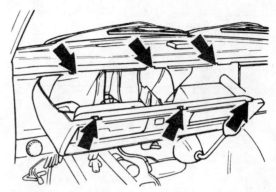

FIG 12:35 Releasing the console. The arrows show the sliding clip positions

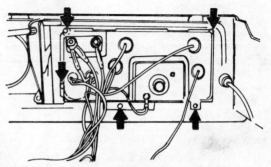

FIG 12:36 Combination instrument assembly fixing screws

FIG 12:37 Instrument retaining tension springs, De Luxe panel

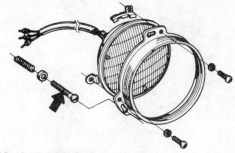

FIG 12:39 Standard headlight unit mounting details, focus adjust screw arrowed

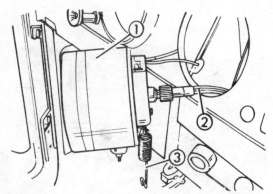

FIG 12:38 Instrument removal, De Luxe panel

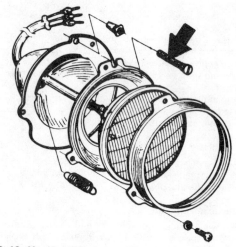

FIG 12:40 Headlight mounting details, USA export models, focus adjusting screw arrowed

The bulb holders for the pilot lamps have bayonet fixings and should be turned anticlockwise for removal. Do not drop the glass when the instrument unit is removed.

Refitting:

This is a reversal of the removal procedure. Check the operation of all instruments and bulbs on completion.

Instrument removal, De Luxe panel:

The speedometer and combination instrument housing are retained in position by tension springs. Release the springs as shown in **FIG 12:37**, then disconnect the wires and the speedometer cable and remove the units as shown in **FIG 12:38**.

Refitting:

This is a reversal of the removal procedure. Check the operation of all instruments and bulbs on completion.

12:8 Headlights

Headlight mounting details are shown in **FIG 12:39** for standard conditions, in **FIG 12:40** for models exported to the USA.

To remove a headlight unit, remove the retaining ring screws without disturbing the beam adjustment screws, arrowed, remove the ring and pull out the unit. Disconnect the connector from the rear of the unit to remove it from the car. Refitting is a reversal of this procedure.

Beam-setting:

Headlamps should be set so that, when the car is normally loaded and the tyre pressures are correct, the main beams are parallel to each other and to the road. Adjustment is by means of the screws provided. Accurate beam-setting is best left to a service station having special optical beam-setting equipment.

12:9 Lighting circuits

Lamps give insufficient light:

Refer to **Section 12:2** and check the condition of the battery, recharging it if necessary. Check the setting of the headlights as described in **Section 12:8** and renew any lamp units or bulbs which have darkened with age.

Bulbs burn out frequently:

Have the control box settings checked by an auto-electrical service station.

Lamps light when switched on but gradually fade:

Refer to **Section 12:2** and check the battery, as it is not capable of supplying current for any length of time.

Lamp brilliance varies with the speed of the car:

Check the condition of the battery and its connections. Make sure that the connections are clean and tight and renew any faulty cables.

12:10 Fault diagnosis

(a) Battery discharged

1 Terminal connections loose or dirty
2 Shorts in lighting circuits
3 Insufficient or zero charge rate
4 Control box faulty
5 Battery internally defective

(b) Insufficient charge rate

1 Check 1 and 4 in (a)
2 Drive belt slipping
3 Alternator diodes defective

(c) Battery will not hold charge

1 Low electrolyte level
2 Battery plates sulphated
3 Electrolyte leakage from cracked case
4 Battery plate separators defective

(d) Battery overcharged

1 Control box faulty

(e) Charge rate low or nil

1 Control box faulty
2 Brushes sticking, springs weak or broken
3 Defective generator or alternator windings
4 Defective alternator diodes

(f) Starter motor lacks power or will not turn

1 Battery discharged, loose cable connections
2 Jammed starter gear
3 Starter switch or solenoid faulty
4 Brushes worn or sticking, leads detached or shorting
5 Commutator dirty or worn
6 Starter shaft bent
7 Engine abnormally stiff, perhaps due to rebore

(g) Starter runs but does not turn engine

1 Starter gears faulty or damaged

(h) Noisy starter when engine running

1 Pinion mechanism faulty
2 Starter mountings loose

(j) Starter motor inoperative

1 Check 1 and 4 in (f)
2 Armature or field coils faulty

(k) Starter motor rough or noisy

1 Mounting bolts loose
2 Pinion mechanism faulty
3 Damaged gear teeth

(l) Lamps inoperative or erratic

1 Battery low, bulbs burned out
2 Faulty earthing of lamps or battery
3 Lighting switch faulty, loose or broken connections

(m) Wiper motor sluggish, taking high current

1 Wiper motor defective internally
2 Lack of lubrication
3 Wiper motor fixings loose

(n) Wiper motor runs but does not drive arms

1 Wiper linkage faulty
2 Wiper transmission components worn

(o) Gauges do not work

1 Check wiring for continuity
2 Check instruments and transmitters for continuity

NOTES

CHAPTER 13

THE BODYWORK

13:1 Bodywork finish

Large scale repairs to body panels are best left to expert panel beaters. Even small dents can be tricky, as too much hammering will stretch the metal and make things worse instead of better. If panel beating is to be attempted, use a dolly on the opposite side of the panel. The head of a large hammer will suffice for small dents, but for large dents a block of metal will be necessary. Use light hammer blows to reshape the panel, pressing the dolly against the opposite side of the panel to absorb the blows. If this method is used to reduce the depth of dents, final smoothing with a suitable filler will be easier, although it may be best to avoid hammering minor dents and just use the filler.

Clean the area to be filled, making sure that it is free from paint, rust and grease, then roughen the area with emerycloth to ensure a good bond. Use a proprietory Fibreglass filler paste mixed according to the manufacturer's instructions and press it into the dent with a putty knife or similar flat-bladed tool. Allow the filler to stand proud of the surrounding area to allow for rubbing down after hardening. Use a file and emerycloth or a disc sander to blend the repaired area to the surrounding bodywork, using finer grade abrasives as the work nears completion. Apply a coat of primer surfacer and, when it is dry, rub down with Wet or Dry paper lubricated with soapy water, finishing with 400 grade. Apply more primer and repeat the operation until the surface is perfectly smooth. Take time on achieving the best finish possible at this stage, as it will control the final effect.

The touching up of paintwork can be carried out with self-spraying cans of paint, these being available in a wide range of colours. Use a piece of newspaper or board as a test panel to practice on first, so that the action of the spray will be familiar when it is used on the panel. Before spraying the panel, remove all traces of wax polish. Mask off large areas such as windows with newspaper and masking tape. Small areas such as trim strips or door handles can be wrapped with masking tape or carefully coated with grease or Vaseline. Apply the touching up paint, spraying with short bursts and keeping the spray moving. Do not attempt to cover the area in one coat, applying several light coats with a few minutes drying time between each. If too much paint is applied at one time, runs may develop. If so, do not try to remove the run by wiping, but wait until it is dry and rub down as before.

After the final coat has been applied, allow a few hours of drying time before blending the new finish to the old

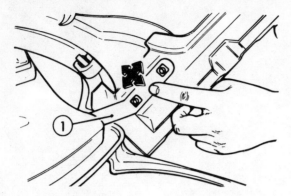

FIG 13:1   Bonnet hinge 1 mountings

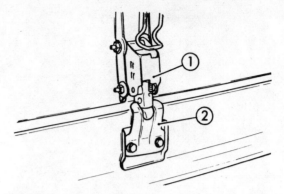

FIG 13:4   Rear compartment lid lock 1 and latch 2 assembly

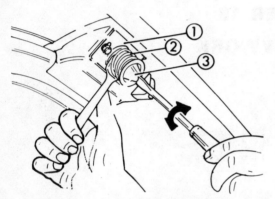

FIG 13:2   Bonnet lock dowel adjustment

FIG 13:5   Front wing mounting bolt locations

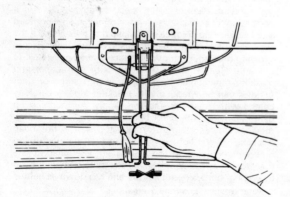

FIG 13:3   Rear compartment lid removal

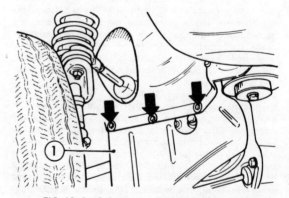

FIG 13:6   Splash guard plate 1 mountings

with a fine cutting compound, buffing with a light, circular motion. Finish with the application of a good quality polish.

13:2 Bonnet and rear compartment lids

Bonnet removal:

The bonnet is removed by taking out the four hinges to bonnet lid bolts, two of each side, which are shown in **FIG 13:1**. When the bonnet is refitted, adjustments can be made to ensure a good fit relative to the surrounding bodywork, by moving the bonnet lid within the limits of the oversize mounting holes provided.

Bonnet lock:

If the bonnet lid does not close properly, adjustments should be made at the dowel 3 shown in **FIG 13:2**. Loosen the locknut 2 and turn the dowel inwards to close the bonnet more tightly, outwards to correct an overtight fit. If the dowel does not fit centrally into the striker plate as the bonnet is closed, loosen the two bolts which secure the dowel assembly 1 to the bonnet and move the assembly as necessary, using the slotted mounting holes provided. Grease the dowel to ensure smooth operation and check the security of the bonnet safety catch.

Rear compartment lid removal:

The rear compartment lid is made from ABS plastic and supported on two hinges. To remove the lid, first release the lid stay by pressing the ends together as shown in **FIG 13:3**, then disconnect the wires at the junction in the illustration. Unscrew the nuts from the hinge mountings on each side of the lid, then remove the mounting washers and separate the lid from the hinges.

Refit in the reverse order of removal, adjusting the fit of the lid against the surrounding bodywork by moving the lid within the limits of the oversize mounting holes provided, before finally tightening the nuts.

Rear compartment lid lock:

Check the rear compartment lid for proper closing by holding the open lid in the horizontal position, then allowing to drop under its own weight. If the lid shuts completely and firmly, operation is correct. If not, the lid lock latch plate should be adjusted. To do this, loosen the bolts securing the lid latch 2 shown in **FIG 13:4**, then move the latch plate downward, or alternatively, leave the bolts tightened and gently bend the latch towards the front of the car by tapping with a hammer.

13:3 Front wing removal

The front wing (fender) panel can be removed from the car body, for access to other components or for renewal if damaged, attachment being by means of bolts at the points shown in **FIG 13:5**. On models fitted with engine-type heater units, a splash guard 1 is fitted as shown in **FIG 13:6**, to prevent water from entering the engine compartment.

13:4 Door components

The door can be removed, if necessary, by removing either the hinge to body bolts or the hinge to door bolts.

FIG 13:7   Door position adjustment

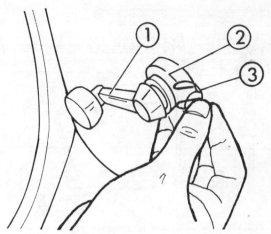

FIG 13:8   Regulator handle removal

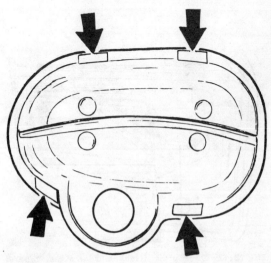

FIG 13:9   The lever housing retaining claws

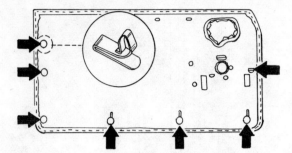

FIG 13:10   Door trim panel retaining clips

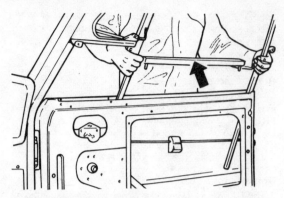

FIG 13:13   Door glass and sash assembly removal

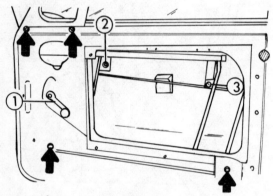

FIG 13:11   Door glass attachment 2 and 3, type A regulator assembly

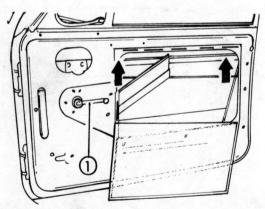

FIG 13:12   Door glass attachment arrowed, type B regulator assembly

However, the door must always be refitted with the hinges attached to the door. Support the door during the removal procedure, to prevent damage.

The door can be adjusted for a proper fit in the body aperture by loosening the appropriate hinge bolts and moving the door as shown in **FIG 13:7**. If this procedure does not provide necessary amount of movement, shims must be added between the hinge and door 2 or between the hinge and body 1.

Dismantling:

Remove the regulator handle 1 and the door lock lever. **FIG 13:8** shows the regulator handle retainer clip 3 which is removed after pushing back the escutcheon 2. The lock lever is retained by a screw.

Remove the lock lever housing, which is attached to the door panel by four claws, as shown in **FIG 13:9**. Insert a flat-bladed screwdriver between the door trim and the door panel, then lever the trim away from the door to release the clips, as shown in **FIG 13:10**. Carefully peel off the vinyl centre seal and retain for re-use.

Disconnect the door glass from the regulator mechanism and remove the five bolts which attach the sash to the door panel. One of two alternative types of regulator mechanism may be fitted, type A being shown in **FIG 13:11** and type B in **FIG 13:12**. Remove the outer weatherstrip from its clips on the panel, then lift out the door glass and sash assembly as shown in **FIG 13:13**. Take care not to drop the glass.

Take out the fixing bolts and remove the regulator mechanism as shown in **FIG 13:14**. The type B regulator mechanism is shown in **FIG 13:15**. Handle the regulator mechanism carefully to avoid distortion, which could make window operation stiff.

Remove the remote control mechanism and the door lock unit as an assembly, as shown in **FIG 13:16**. Retain the piece of sponge rubber 2 which is fitted to prevent the remote control rod 1 from vibrating.

Reassembly:

This is a reversal of the dismantling procedure, noting the following points:

Apply a thin coat of grease to the moving parts of the door lock and window regulator assemblies. When the door glass and sash assembly is refitted, check the action

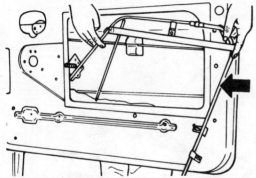

FIG 13:14 Regulator mechanism removal, type A shown

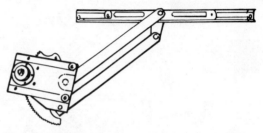

FIG 13:15 Type B regulator mechanism

of the ventilator glass and, if necessary, adjust the action with the nut provided at the pivot mounting. Make sure that the vinyl centre seal is properly refitted without wrinkles or loose edges.

13:5 Windscreen glass

Removal:

If the windscreen is to be removed intact, pull the wiper arms away from the glass so that they lock in the raised position, then carefully push out the glass. Have an assistant steady the glass to prevent damage to the glass or the bonnet. If the screen has been broken, carefully push out the main areas, using a dust sheet to protect the paintwork. Remove the weatherstrip and clean out all broken glass.

Installation:

Clean the windscreen aperture flange and the weatherstrip. If the weatherstrip is cracked or perished it should be renewed, or water leakage may occur.

Install the weatherstrip to the windscreen glass and pass a length of cord, approximately 6mm (0.236in) in diameter, around the full length of the weatherstrip in the aperture flange groove. Cross the ends of the cord at the bottom centre of the windscreen, then offer the assembly into position from the outside, as shown in **FIG 13:17**.

Have an assistant push the glass firmly from the outside, then pull out the cord to lip the weatherstrip over the aperture flange. Work evenly on both sides, not at one side then the other. When the cord has been removed at the top centre of the screen, check all round for proper installation. Fit the moulding retaining clip at the top centre of the weatherstrip.

13:6 The heater

The heater unit may be either of two types, engine or exhaust. The engine type heater uses engine cooling air to warm the interior of the car, the exhaust type uses fresh air passing through an exhaust pipe heat exchanger with the flow assisted by a blower unit.

Engine type heater:

The layout of this system is shown in **FIG 13:18**.

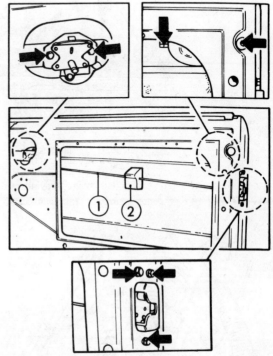

FIG 13:16 Lock and remote control mechanism removal

FIG 13:17 Fitting windscreen glass

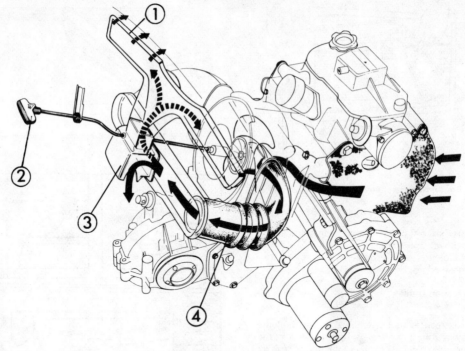

FIG 13:18   Layout of the engine-type heater system

Key to Fig 13:18   1 Defroster nozzle   2 Control handle   3 Control valve housing   4 Hot air duct

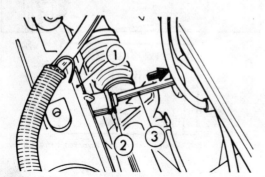

FIG 13:19   Disconnecting the heater control rod 3

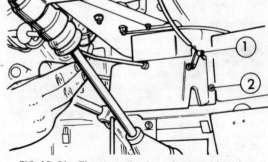

FIG 13:21   The control valve wire 1 and housing

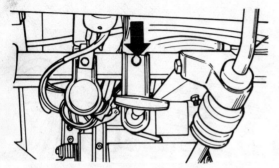

FIG 13:20   Removing the control lever bracket

FIG 13:22   Removing the heater control knob 1

Removal:

Refer to **FIG 13:19** and pull out the heater control rod joint pin 2 to disconnect the rod 3 from the heater drum 1, then force the rod towards the interior of the car. Remove the control lever bracket, then remove the rod from the housing, as shown in **FIG 13:20**. Loosen the screw 1 shown in **FIG 13:21** and disconnect the control wire. Remove the two fixing screws 2 and remove the control valve housing.

Take out the screw shown in **FIG 13:22** and separate the control lever knob 1 from the control lever. Remove the two screws shown in **FIG 13:23** to detach the control lever assembly from the back of the instrument panel.

Refitting:

This is a reversal of the removal procedure. On completion, run the engine and check the operation of the heater.

Exhaust type heater:

The layout of this system is shown in **FIG 13:24**.

FIG 13:23   Removing the heater control assembly

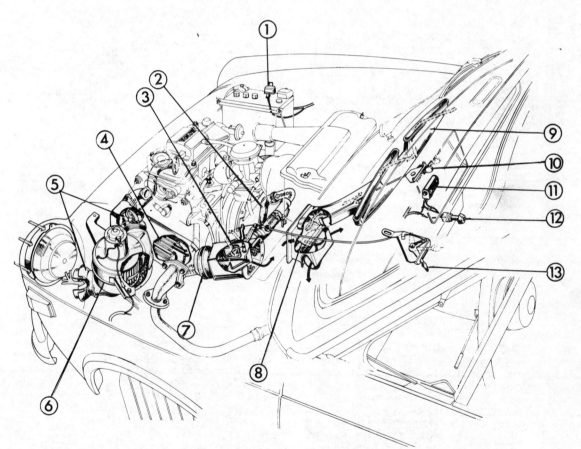

FIG 13:24   Layout of the exhaust-type heater system

Key to Fig 13:24   1 Idle stop relay   2 Hot air discharge duct   3 Control valve   4 Heat exchanger   5 Air inlet ducts   6 Blower   7 Hot air duct   8 Control valve   9 Defroster nozzle   10 Defroster control lever   11 Resistor   12 Heater switch   13 Heater control lever

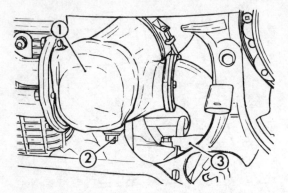

FIG 13:25   Heat exchanger mountings

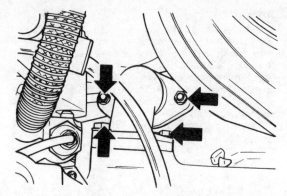

FIG 13:28   Exhaust pipe flange bolts

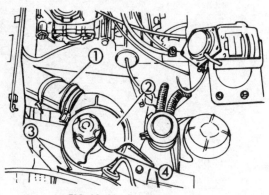

FIG 13:26   Blower removal

FIG 13:29   Heater control mountings, De Luxe instrument panel

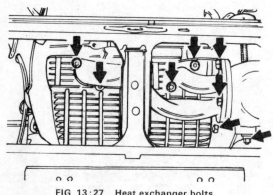

FIG 13:27   Heat exchanger bolts

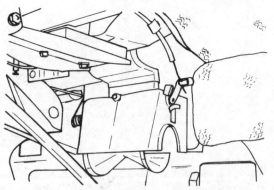

FIG 13:30   Heater control valve housing

Heat exchanger and blower removal:

The heat exchanger 1 is connected to the exhaust pipes by flanges and supported at the bottom 2, as shown in **FIG 13:25**. Refer to **FIG 13:26** and remove air inlet duct B1. Disconnect the electrical lead 4, then remove the blower assembly 2, disconnecting it from duct A3 while doing so.

Refitting:

This is a reversal of the removal procedure, noting the following points:

Discard all gaskets and use new gaskets whenever the heat exchanger or exhaust pipes are installed. It is also recommended that the lower exhaust pipe flange be renewed, as this part may be distorted in service. Check the mounting bolts shown in **FIGS 13:27** and **13:28** carefully to avoid gas leaks. The exhaust pipes and heat exchanger units should always be loosely mounted, then the nuts and bolts tightened evenly and alternately, working from the front of the car towards the rear. This will prevent strain on the components in service. The 8mm nuts and bolts should be tightened to a torque of 2.0 to 2.4kgm (14 to 18lb ft), the 10mm nuts and bolts to 4.0 to 4.8kgm (29 to 35lb ft).

Heater control removal:

Loosen the screw and remove the control knob from the control lever on the instrument panel. Remove the two screws shown in **FIG 13:23** or **13:29** to separate

FIG 13:31   Heater control cable adjustment

the control unit from the rear of the instrument panel. Refitting is a reversal of the removal procedure.

Heater control valve housing removal:

Loosen the screw and detach the control wire, then remove the two mounting screws and remove the housing assembly as shown in **FIG 13:30**. Refitting is a reversal of the removal procedure.

Control cable adjustment:

Refer to **FIG 13:31**. Adjust the cable 1 in the 'shut' position. Shut the valve by hand, position the cable control lever correctly, then adjust the cable for proper operation at the cable connection.

NOTES

APPENDIX

TECHNICAL DATA

HINTS ON MAINTENANCE AND OVERHAUL

GLOSSARY OF TERMS

INDEX

Inches		Decimals	Milli-metres	Inches to Millimetres		Millimetres to Inches	
				Inches	mm	mm	Inches
	1/64	.015625	.3969	.001	.0254	.01	.00039
1/32		.03125	.7937	.002	.0508	.02	.00079
	3/64	.046875	1.1906	.003	.0762	.03	.00118
1/16		.0625	1.5875	.004	.1016	.04	.00157
	5/64	.078125	1.9844	.005	.1270	.05	.00197
3/32		.09375	2.3812	.006	.1524	.06	.00236
	7/64	.109375	2.7781	.007	.1778	.07	.00276
1/8		.125	3.1750	.008	.2032	.08	.00315
	9/64	.140625	3.5719	.009	.2286	.09	.00354
5/32		.15625	3.9687	.01	.254	.1	.00394
	11/64	.171875	4.3656	.02	.508	.2	.00787
3/16		.1875	4.7625	.03	.762	.3	.01181
	13/64	.203125	5·1594	.04	1.016	.4	.01575
7/32		.21875	5.5562	.05	1.270	.5	.01969
	15/64	.234375	5.9531	.06	1.524	.6	.02362
1/4		.25	6.3500	.07	1.778	.7	.02756
	17/64	.265625	6.7469	.08	2.032	.8	.03150
9/32		.28125	7.1437	.09	2.286	.9	.03543
	19/64	.296875	7.5406	.1	2.54	1	.03937
5/16		.3125	7.9375	.2	5.08	2	.07874
	21/64	.328125	8.3344	.3	7.62	3	.11811
11/32		.34375	8.7312	.4	10.16	4	.15748
	23/64	.359375	9.1281	.5	12.70	5	.19685
3/8		.375	9.5250	.6	15.24	6	.23622
	25/64	.390625	9.9219	.7	17.78	7	.27559
13/32		.40625	10.3187	.8	20.32	8	.31496
	27/64	.421875	10.7156	.9	22.86	9	.35433
7/16		.4375	11.1125	1	25.4	10	.39370
	29/64	.453125	11.5094	2	50.8	11	.43307
15/32		.46875	11.9062	3	76.2	12	.47244
	31/64	.484375	12.3031	4	101.6	13	.51181
1/2		.5	12.7000	5	127.0	14	.55118
	33/64	.515625	13.0969	6	152.4	15	.59055
17/32		.53125	13.4937	7	177.8	16	.62992
	35/64	.546875	13.8906	8	203.2	17	.66929
9/16		.5625	14.2875	9	228.6	18	.70866
	37/64	.578125	14.6844	10	254.0	19	.74803
19/32		.59375	15.0812	11	279.4	20	.78740
	39/64	.609375	15.4781	12	304.8	21	.82677
5/8		.625	15.8750	13	330.2	22	.86614
	41/64	.640625	16.2719	14	355.6	23	.90551
21/32		.65625	16.6687	15	381.0	24	.94488
	43/64	.671875	17.0656	16	406.4	25	.98425
11/16		.6875	17.4625	17	431.8	26	1.02362
	45/64	.703125	17.8594	18	457.2	27	1.06299
23/32		.71875	18.2562	19	482.6	28	1.10236
	47/64	.734375	18.6531	20	508.0	29	1.14173
3/4		.75	19.0500	21	533.4	30	1.18110
	49/64	.765625	19.4469	22	558.8	31	1.22047
25/32		.78125	19.8437	23	584.2	32	1.25984
	51/64	.796875	20.2406	24	609.6	33	1.29921
13/16		.8125	20.6375	25	635.0	34	1.33858
	53/64	.828125	21.0344	26	660.4	35	1.37795
27/32		.84375	21.4312	27	685.8	36	1.41732
	55/64	.859375	21.8281	28	711.2	37	1.4567
7/8		.875	22.2250	29	736.6	38	1.4961
	57/64	.890625	22.6219	30	762.0	39	1.5354
29/32		.90625	23.0187	31	787.4	40	1.5748
	59/64	.921875	23.4156	32	812.8	41	1.6142
15/16		.9375	23.8125	33	838.2	42	1.6535
	61/64	.953125	24.2094	34	863.6	43	1.6929
31/32		.96875	24.6062	35	889.0	44	1.7323
	63/64	.984375	25.0031	36	914.4	45	1.7717

UNITS	Pints to Litres	Gallons to Litres	Litres to Pints	Litres to Gallons	Miles to Kilometres	Kilometres to Miles	Lbs. per sq. In. to Kg. per sq. Cm.	Kg. per sq. Cm. to Lbs. per sq. In.
1	.57	4.55	1.76	.22	1.61	.62	.07	14.22
2	1.14	9.09	3.52	.44	3.22	1.24	.14	28.50
3	1.70	13.64	5.28	.66	4.83	1.86	.21	42.67
4	2.27	18.18	7.04	.88	6.44	2.49	.28	56.89
5	2.84	22.73	8.80	1.10	8.05	3.11	.35	71.12
6	3.41	27.28	10.56	1.32	9.66	3.73	.42	85.34
7	3.98	31.82	12.32	1.54	11.27	4.35	.49	99.56
8	4.55	36.37	14.08	1.76	12.88	4.97	.56	113.79
9		40.91	15.84	1.98	14.48	5.59	.63	128.00
10		45.46	17.60	2.20	16.09	6.21	.70	142.23
20				4.40	32.19	12.43	1.41	284.47
30				6.60	48.28	18.64	2.11	426.70
40				8.80	64.37	24.85		
50					80.47	31.07		
60					96.56	37.28		
70					112.65	43.50		
80					128.75	49.71		
90					144.84	55.92		
100					160.93	62.14		

UNITS	Lb ft to kgm	Kgm to lb ft	UNITS	Lb ft to kgm	Kgm to lb ft
1	.138	7.233	7	.967	50.631
2	.276	14.466	8	1.106	57.864
3	.414	21.699	9	1.244	65.097
4	.553	28.932	10	1.382	72.330
5	.691	36.165	20	2.765	144.660
6	.829	43.398	30	4.147	216.990

TECHNICAL DATA

Dimensions given are in millimetres with inches in brackets unless otherwise stated

ENGINE

Type	Forced air-cooled, four stroke, two cylinder
Bore and stroke:	
360	62.5 × 57.8 (2.46 × 2.28)
600	74 × 69.6 (2.91 × 2.74)
Displacement:	
360	354.0cc (21.4cu in)
600	598.4cc (36.5cu in)
Compression ratio:	
360	8.6:1
600	8.3:1
Compression pressure (at cranking speed):	
360	12 ± 0.5kg/sq cm (170 ± 7lb/sq in)
600	11 ± 0.5kg/sq cm (156 ± 7lb/sq in)

Pistons:

Type	Offset pin, cast alloy aluminium
Diameters:	
Top land, 360	61.95 to 62.00 (2.4390 to 2.4410)
600	73.40 to 73.45 (2.8900 to 2.8910)
Skirt, 360	62.45 to 62.47 (2.4580 to 2.4590)
600	73.95 to 73.97 (2.9111 to 2.9120)
Piston rings:	
Type	Two compression and one oil control
Clearances:	
Side clearance, top ring	0.045 to 0.075 (0.0018 to 0.0030)
middle and oil control rings ..	0.015 to 0.045 (0.0006 to 0.0018)
End gap (all rings)	0.2 to 0.4 (0.008 to 0.015)
Piston pin:	
Piston pin bore (in piston)	17.002 to 17.008 (0.6694 to 0.6696)
Piston pin diameter	16.994 to 17.000 (0.6691 to 0.6693)

Crankshaft:

Type	Forged steel with integral connecting rod assemblies and press-fitted needle roller bearings at the main and big-end journals

Connecting rods:

Small-end bore serviceable limit	17.043 (0.6709)
Big-end side (axial) clearance	0.12 to 0.33 (0.0047 to 0.0130)
serviceable limit	0.49 (0.0193)
Big-end radial clearance	0 to 0.01 (0 to 0.0004)
serviceable limit ..	0.04 (0.0016)

Note that main bearings are also of the roller bearing type, having the same clearances and limits as those given for big-end bearings. Only the two outer main bearings are renewable, the inner ones, when worn, dictate crankshaft renewal, as do the connecting rods big- and small-ends.

Oil pump:

Type	Pluger (manual transmission), or Trochoid (automatic transmission)
Delivery rate:	
Plunger type	3.1 litre/min (5.45 pint/min) at 2800rev/min engine speed
Trochoid type	5.5 litre/min (9.6 pint/min) at 5000rev/min engine speed
Oil filter type	Paper element

Valves:

Valve seat angle (inlet and exhaust)	45°
Valve seat width (inlet and exhaust)	0.8 to 1.0 (0.032 to 0.040)
Valve stem diameter, inlet	6.58 to 6.59 (0.2591 to 0.2594)
exhaust	6.55 to 6.56 (0.2579 to 0.2583)
Valve head rim thickness, inlet	0.9 to 1.0 (0.0350 to 0.0433)
exhaust	1.4 to 1.6 (0.0550 to 0.0630)

Valve stem to guide clearance:

Inlet	0.01 to 0.04 (0.0004 to 0.0016)
Exhaust	0.04 to 0.07 (0.0016 to 0.0028)

Valve springs:

Free length, inner	42.0 (1.65)
outer	44.8 (1.76)

Valve timing (360):

Inlet opens	TDC
Inlet closes	30° ABDC
Exhaust opens	40° BBDC
Exhaust closes	TDC

Valve timing (600):

Inlet opens	TDC (5° BTDC, models from 1970)
Inlet closes	40° ABDC (20° ABDC, from 1970)
Exhaust opens	40° BBDC (all models)
Exhaust closes	TDC (10° ATDC, from 1970)
Valve operating clearance (inlet and exhaust) ..	0.08 to 0.12 (0.003 to 0.005), cold

Camshaft:

Lobe height (heel to toe):

360 inlet cam lobe	39.73 to 40.89 (1.566 to 1.610)
exhaust cam lobe	40.25 to 40.41 (1.585 to 1.591)
600 inlet cam lobe	41.21 to 41.37 (1.622 to 1.629)
exhaust cam lobe	40.73 to 40.89 (1.604 to 1.610)

Note that the camshaft must be renewed if any lobe is 0.03mm (0.002in) below the minimum dimensions given.

FUEL SYSTEM

Fuel pump:

Type	Electric, 12 volt, 0.6amp
Discharge capacity	More than 250cc/min

Carburetter specifications (360):

Index Mark	Main jet Secondary	Primary	Air jet Secondary	Primary	Needle jet	Idle jet	Idle air jet	Float level (mm)	Accelerator Pump Vol/stroke (cc)	Stroke (mm)	Pilot screw
NE	145	80	90	50	223302	35	90	17	0.25 ± 0.05	2.4 ± 0.5	$\frac{3}{4}$
NF	145	80	90	50	223302	35	80	17	0.20 ± 0.05	2.4 ± 0.5	$\frac{5}{8}$
NH	135	82	90	50	223303	35	80	17	0.20 ± 0.05	1.6 ± 0.5	$\frac{5}{8}$
NI	135	82	90	50	223303	35	80	17	0.20 ± 0.05	2.3 ± 0.5	$\frac{5}{8}$
NJ	135	82	90	50	223303	35	100	17	0.20 ± 0.05	2.3 ± 0.5	$\frac{5}{8}$

Carburetter specification (600):

Index Mark	Main jet Secondary	Primary	Air jet Secondary	Primary	Needle jet	Idle jet	Idle air jet	Float level (mm)	Accelerator Pump Vol/stroke (cc)	Stroke (mm)	Pilot screw
N6B	150	85	70	70	234301	35	120	16	0.20 ± 0.05	1.6 ± 0.5	$1\frac{1}{4}$
N6C	140	88	50	50	234002	35	120	16	0.35 ± 0.05	2.8 ± 0.5	$1\frac{1}{4}$
N6D	140	88	50	50	234003	35	120	16	0.20 ± 0.05	1.6 ± 0.5	$1\frac{1}{4}$
N6D1	140	88	50	50	224003	35	120	22	0.20 ± 0.05	2.3 ± 0.5	$2\frac{1}{8}$
N6D2	140	88	50	50	224003	35	120	22	0.20 ± 0.05	2.3 ± 0.5	$2\frac{1}{8}$
6NM	135	92	90	50	—	6	130	23.5	0.30	2.3 ± 0.5	$1\frac{1}{4}$

IGNITION SYSTEM

Distributor:

Type	Rotorless, with vacuum and centrifugal advance mechanisms
Contact points gap	0.3 to 0.4 (0.012 to 0.015)

HINTS ON MAINTENANCE AND OVERHAUL

There are few things more rewarding than the restoration of a vehicle's original peak of efficiency and smooth performance.

The following notes are intended to help the owner to reach that state of perfection. Providing that he possesses the basic manual skills he should have no difficulty in performing most of the operations detailed in this manual. It must be stressed, however, that where recommended in the manual, highly-skilled operations ought to be entrusted to experts, who have the necessary equipment, to carry out the work satisfactorily.

Quality of workmanship:

The hazardous driving conditions on the roads to-day demand that vehicles should be as nearly perfect, mechanically, as possible. It is therefore most important that amateur work be carried out with care, bearing in mind the often inadequate working conditions, and also the inferior tools which may have to be used. It is easy to counsel perfection in all things, and we recognise that it may be setting an impossibly high standard. We do, however, suggest that every care should be taken to ensure that a vehicle is as safe to take on the road as it is humanly possible to make it.

Safe working conditions:

Even though a vehicle may be stationary, it is still potentially dangerous if certain sensible precautions are not taken when working on it while it is supported on jacks or blocks. It is indeed preferable not to use jacks alone, but to supplement them with carefully placed blocks, so that there will be plenty of support if the car rolls off the jacks during a strenuous manoeuvre. Axle stands are an excellent way of providing a rigid base which is not readily disturbed. Piles of bricks are a dangerous substitute. Be careful not to get under heavy loads on lifting tackle, the load could fall. It is preferable not to work alone when lifting an engine, or when working underneath a vehicle which is supported well off the ground. To be trapped, particularly under the vehicle, may have unpleasant results if help is not quickly forthcoming. Make some provision, however humble, to deal with fires. Always disconnect a battery if there is a likelihood of electrical shorts. These may start a fire if there is leaking fuel about. This applies particularly to leads which can carry a heavy current, like those in the starter circuit. While on the subject of electricity, we must also stress the danger of using equipment which is run off the mains and which has no earth or has faulty wiring or connections. So many workshops have damp floors, and electrical shocks are of such a nature that it is sometimes impossible to let go of a live lead or piece of equipment due to the muscular spasms which take place.

Work demanding special care:

This involves the servicing of braking, steering and suspension systems. On the road, failure of the braking system may be disastrous. Make quite sure that there can be no possibility of failure through the bursting of rusty brake pipes or rotten hoses, nor to a sudden loss of pressure due to defective seals or valves.

Problems:

The chief problems which may face an operator are:

1 External dirt.
2 Difficulty in undoing tight fixings.
3 Dismantling unfamiliar mechanisms.
4 Deciding in what respect parts are defective.
5 Confusion about the correct order for reassembly.
6 Adjusting running clearance.
7 Road testing.
8 Final tuning.

Practical suggestions to solve the problems:

1 Preliminary cleaning of large parts—engines, transmissions, steering, suspensions, etc,—should be carried out before removal from the car. Where road dirt and mud alone are present, wash clean with a high-pressure water jet, brushing to remove stubborn adhesions, and allow to drain and dry. Where oil or grease is also present, wash down with a proprietary compound (Gunk, Teepol etc,) applying with a stiff brush—an old paint brush is suitable—into all crevices. Cover the distributor and ignition coils with a polythene bag and then apply a strong water jet to clear the loosened deposits. Allow to drain and dry. The assemblies will then be sufficiently clean to remove and transfer to the bench for the next stage.

On the bench, further cleaning can be carried out, first wiping the parts as free as possible from grease with old newspaper. Avoid using rag or cotton waste which can leave clogging fibres behind. Any remaining grease can be removed with a brush dipped in paraffin. If necessary, traces of paraffin can be removed by carbon tetrachloride. Avoid using paraffin or petrol in large quantities for cleaning in enclosed areas, such as garages, on account of the high fire risk.

When all exteriors have been cleaned, and not before, dismantling can be commenced. This ensures that dirt will not enter into interiors and orifices revealed by dismantling. In the next phases, where components have to be cleaned, use carbon tetrachloride in preference to petrol and keep the containers covered except when in use. After the components have been cleaned, plug small holes with tapered hard wood plugs cut to size and blank off larger orifices with grease-proof paper and masking tape. Do not use soft wood plugs or matchsticks as they may break.

2 It is not advisable to hammer on the end of a screw thread, but if it must be done, first screw on a nut to protect the thread, and use a lead hammer. This applies particularly to the removal of tapered cotters. Nuts and bolts seem to 'grow' together, especially in exhaust systems. If penetrating oil does not work, try the judicious application of heat, but be careful of starting a fire. Asbestos sheet or cloth is useful to isolate heat.

Tight bushes or pieces of tail-pipe rusted into a silencer can be removed by splitting them with an open-ended hacksaw. Tight screws can sometimes be started by a tap from a hammer on the end of a suitable screwdriver. Many tight fittings will yield to the judicious use of a hammer, but it must be a soft-faced hammer if damage is to be avoided, use a heavy block on the opposite side to absorb shock. Any parts of the steering system which have been damaged should be renewed, as attempts to repair them may lead to cracking and subsequent failure, and steering ball joints should be disconnected using a recommended tool to prevent damage.

3 It often happens that an owner is baffled when trying to dismantle an unfamiliar piece of equipment. So many modern devices are pressed together or assembled by spinning-over flanges, that they must be sawn apart. The intention is that the whole assembly must be renewed. However, parts which appear to be in one piece to the naked eye, may reveal close-fitting joint lines when inspected with a magnifying glass, and, this may provide the necessary clue to dismantling. Lefthanded screw threads are used where rotational forces would tend to unscrew a righthanded screw thread.

Be very careful when dismantling mechanisms which may come apart suddenly. Work in an enclosed space where the parts will be contained, and drape a piece of cloth over the device if springs are likely to fly in all directions. Mark everything which might be reassembled in the wrong position, scratched symbols may be used on unstressed parts, or a sequence of tiny dots from a centre punch can be useful. Stressed parts should never be scratched or centre-popped as this may lead to cracking under working conditions. Store parts which look alike in the correct order for reassembly. Never rely upon memory to assist in the assembly of complicated mechanisms, especially when they will be dismantled for a long time, but make notes, and drawings to supplement the diagrams in the manual, and put labels on detached wires. Rust stains may indicate unlubricated wear. This can sometimes be seen round the outside edge of a bearing cup in a universal joint. Look for bright rubbing marks on parts which normally should not make heavy contact. These might prove that something is bent or running out of truth. For example, there might be bright marks on one side of a piston, at the top near the ring grooves, and others at the bottom of the skirt on the other side. This could well be the clue to a bent connecting rod. Suspected cracks can be proved by heating the component in a light oil to approximately 100°C, removing, drying off, and dusting with french chalk, if a crack is present the oil retained in the crack will stain the french chalk.

4 In determining wear, and the degree, against the permissible limits set in the manual, accurate measurement can only be achieved by the use of a micrometer. In many cases, the wear is given to the fourth place of decimals; that is in ten-thousandths of an inch. This can be read by the vernier scale on the barrel of a good micrometer. Bore diameters are more difficult to determine. If, however, the matching shaft is accurately measured, the degree of play in the bore can be felt as a guide to its suitability. In other cases, the shank of a twist drill of known diameter is a handy check.

Many methods have been devised for determining the clearance between bearing surfaces. To-day the best and simplest is by the use of Plastigage, obtainable from most garages. A thin plastic thread is laid between the two surfaces and the bearing is tightened, flattening the thread. On removal, the width of the thread is compared with a scale supplied with the thread and the clearance is read off directly. Sometimes joint faces leak persistently, even after gasket renewal. The fault will then be traceable to distortion, dirt or burrs. Studs which are screwed into soft metal frequently raise burrs at the point of entry. A quick cure for this is to chamfer the edge of the hole in the part which fits over the stud.

5 **Always check a replacement part with the original one before it is fitted.**

If parts are not marked, and the order for reassembly is not known, a little detective work will help. Look for marks which are due to wear to see if they can be mated. Joint faces may not be identical due to manufacturing errors, and parts which overlap may be stained, giving a clue to the correct position. Most fixings leave identifying marks especially if they were painted over on assembly. It is then easier to decide whether a nut, for instance, has a plain, a spring, or a shakeproof washer under it. All running surfaces become 'bedded' together after long spells of work and tiny imperfections on one part will be found to have left corresponding marks on the other. This is particularly true of shafts and bearings and even a score on a cylinder wall will show on the piston.

6 Checking end float or rocker clearances by feeler gauge may not always give accurate results because of wear. For instance, the rocker tip which bears on a valve stem may be deeply pitted, in which case the feeler will simply be bridging a depression. Thrust washers may also wear depressions in opposing faces to make accurate measurement difficult. End float is then easier to check by using a dial gauge. It is common practice to adjust end play in bearing assemblies, like front hubs with taper rollers, by doing up the axle nut until the hub becomes stiff to turn and then backing it off a little. Do not use this method with ballbearing hubs as the assembly is often preloaded by tightening the axle nut to its fullest extent. If the splitpin hole will not line up, file the base of the nut a little.

Steering assemblies often wear in the straight-ahead position. If any part is adjusted, make sure that it remains free when moved from lock to lock. Do not be surprised if an assembly like a steering gearbox, which is known to be carefully adjusted outside the car, becomes stiff when it is bolted in place. This will be due to distortion of the case by the pull of the mounting bolts, particularly if the mounting points are not all touching together. This problem may be met in other equipment and is cured by careful attention to the alignment of mounting points.

When a spanner is stamped with a size and A/F it means that the dimension is the width between the jaws and has no connection with ANF, which is the designation for the American National Fine thread. Coarse threads like Whitworth are rarely used on cars to-day except for studs which screw into soft aluminium or cast iron. For this reason it might be found that the top end of a cylinder head stud has a fine thread and the lower end a coarse thread to screw into the cylinder block. If the car has mainly UNF threads then it is likely that any coarse threads will be UNC, which are not the same as Whitworth. Small sizes have the same number of threads in Whitworth and UNC, but in the $\frac{1}{2}$ inch size for example, there are twelve threads to the inch in the former and thirteen in the latter.

7 After a major overhaul, particularly if a great deal of work has been done on the braking, steering and suspension systems, it is advisable to approach the problem of testing with care. If the braking system has been overhauled, apply heavy pressure to the brake pedal and get a second operator to check every possible source of leakage. The brakes may work extremely well, but a leak could cause complete failure after a few miles.

Do not fit the hub caps until every wheel nut has been checked for tightness, and make sure the tyre pressures are correct. Check the levels of coolant, lubricants and hydraulic fluids. Being satisfied that all is well, take the car on the road and test the brakes at once. Check the steering and the action of the handbrake. Do all this at moderate speeds on quiet roads, and make sure there is no other vehicle behind you when you try a rapid stop.

Finally, remember that many parts settle down after a time, so check for tightness of all fixings after the car has been on the road for a hundred miles or so.

8 It is useless to tune an engine which has not reached its normal running temperature. In the same way, the tune of an engine which is stiff after a rebore will be different when the engine is again running free. Remember too, that rocker clearances on pushrod operated valve gear will change when the cylinder head nuts are tightened after an initial period of running with a new head gasket.

Trouble may not always be due to what seems the obvious cause. Ignition, carburation and mechanical condition are interdependent and spitting back through the carburetter, which might be attributed to a weak mixture, can be caused by a sticking inlet valve.

For one final hint on tuning, never adjust more than one thing at a time or it will be impossible to tell which adjustment produced the desired result.

NOTES

GLOSSARY OF TERMS

Allen key — Cranked wrench of hexagonal section for use with socket head screws.

Alternator — Electrical generator producing alternating current. Rectified to direct current for battery charging.

Ambient temperature — Surrounding atmospheric temperature.

Annulus — Used in engineering to indicate the outer ring gear of an epicyclic gear train.

Armature — The shaft carrying the windings, which rotates in the magnetic field of a generator or starter motor. That part of a solenoid or relay which is activated by the magnetic field.

Axial — In line with, or pertaining to, an axis.

Backlash — Play in meshing gears.

Balance lever — A bar where force applied at the centre is equally divided between connections at the ends.

Banjo axle — Axle casing with large diameter housing for the crownwheel and differential.

Bendix pinion — A self-engaging and self-disengaging drive on a starter motor shaft.

Bevel pinion — A conical shaped gearwheel, designed to mesh with a similar gear with an axis usually at 90 deg. to its own.

bhp — Brake horse power, measured on a dynamometer.

bmep — Brake mean effective pressure. Average pressure on a piston during the working stroke.

Brake cylinder — Cylinder with hydraulically operated piston(s) acting on brake shoes or pad(s).

Brake regulator — Control valve fitted in hydraulic braking system which limits brake pressure to rear brakes during heavy braking to prevent rear wheel locking.

Camber — Angle at which a wheel is tilted from the vertical.

Capacitor — Modern term for an electrical condenser. Part of distributor assembly, connected across contact breaker points, acts as an interference suppressor.

Castellated — Top face of a nut, slotted across the flats, to take a locking splitpin.

Castor — Angle at which the kingpin or swivel pin is tilted when viewed from the side.

cc — Cubic centimetres. Engine capacity is arrived at by multiplying the area of the bore in sq cm by the stroke in cm by the number of cylinders.

Clevis — U-shaped forked connector used with a clevis pin, usually at handbrake connections.

Collet — A type of collar, usually split and located in a groove in a shaft, and held in place by a retainer. The arrangement used to retain the spring(s) on a valve stem in most cases.

Commutator — Rotating segmented current distributor between armature windings and brushes in generator or motor.

Compression ratio — The ratio, or quantitative relation, of the total volume (piston at bottom of stroke) to the unswept volume (piston at top of stroke) in an engine cylinder.

Condenser — See 'Capacitor'.

Core plug — Plug for blanking off a manufacturing hole in a casting.

Crownwheel — Large bevel gear in rear axle, driven by a bevel pinion attached to the propeller shaft. Sometimes called a 'ring gear'.

'C'-spanner — Like a 'C' with a handle. For use on screwed collars without flats, but with slots or holes.

Damper — Modern term for shock absorber, used in vehicle suspension systems to damp out spring oscillations.

Depression — The lowering of atmospheric pressure as in the inlet manifold and carburetter.

Dowel — Close tolerance pin, peg, tube, or bolt, which accurately locates mating parts.

Drag link — Rod connecting steering box drop arm (pitman arm) to nearest front wheel steering arm in certain types of steering systems.

Dry liner — Thinwall tube pressed into cylinder bore.

Dry sump — Lubrication system where all oil is scavenged from the sump, and returned to a separate tank.

Dynamo — See 'Generator'.

Electrode — Terminal part of an electrical component, such as the points or 'Electrodes' of a sparking plug.

Electrolyte — In lead-acid car batteries a solution of sulphuric acid and distilled water.

End float — The axial movement between associated parts, end play.

EP — Extreme pressure. In lubricants, special grades for heavily loaded bearing surfaces, such as gear teeth in a gearbox, or crownwheel and pinion in a rear axle.

Fade	Of brakes. Reduced efficiency due to overheating.	**Journals**	Those parts of a shaft that are in contact with the bearings.
Field coils	Windings on the polepieces of motors and generators.	**Kingpin**	The main vertical pin which carries the front wheel spindle, and permits steering movement. May be called 'steering pin' or 'swivel pin'.
Fillets	Narrow finishing strips usually applied to interior bodywork.		
First motion shaft	Input shaft from clutch to gearbox.	**Layshaft**	The shaft which carries the laygear in the gearbox. The laygear is driven by the first motion shaft and drives the third motion shaft according to the gear selected. Sometimes called the 'countershaft' or 'second motion shaft'.
Fullflow filter	Filters in which all the oil is pumped to the engine. If the element becomes clogged, a bypass valve operates to pass unfiltered oil to the engine.		
FWD	Front wheel drive.	**lb ft**	A measure of twist or torque. A pull of 10 lb at a radius of 1 ft is a torque of 10 lb ft.
Gear pump	Two meshing gears in a close fitting casing. Oil is carried from the inlet round the outside of both gears in the spaces between the gear teeth and casing to the outlet, the meshing gear teeth prevent oil passing back to the inlet, and the oil is forced through the outlet port.		
		lb/sq in	Pounds per square inch.
		Little-end	The small, or piston end of a connecting rod. Sometimes called the 'small-end'.
		LT	Low Tension. The current output from the battery.
Generator	Modern term for 'Dynamo'. When rotated produces electrical current.	**Mandrel**	Accurately manufactured bar or rod used for test or centring purposes.
Grommet	A ring of protective or sealing material. Can be used to protect pipes or leads passing through bulkheads.	**Manifold**	A pipe, duct, or chamber, with several branches.
		Needle rollers	Bearing rollers with a length many times their diameter.
Grubscrew	Fully threaded headless screw with screwdriver slot. Used for locking, or alignment purposes.	**Oil bath**	Reservoir which lubricates parts by immersion. In air filters, a separate oil supply for wetting a wire mesh element to hold the dust.
Gudgeon pin	Shaft which connects a piston to its connecting rod. Sometimes called 'wrist pin', or 'piston pin'.		
		Oil wetted	In air filters, a wire mesh element lightly oiled to trap and hold airborne dust.
Halfshaft	One of a pair transmitting drive from the differential.		
Helical	In spiral form. The teeth of helical gears are cut at a spiral angle to the side faces of the gearwheel.	**Overlap**	Period during which inlet and exhaust valves are open together.
		Panhard rod	Bar connected between fixed point on chassis and another on axle to control sideways movement.
Hot pot	Hot area that assists vapourisation of fuel on its way to cylinders. Often provided by close contact between inlet and exhaust manifolds.		
		Pawl	Pivoted catch which engages in the teeth of a ratchet to permit movement in one direction only.
HT	High Tension. Applied to electrical current produced by the ignition coil for the sparking plugs.	**Peg spanner**	Tool with pegs, or pins, to engage in holes or slots in the part to be turned.
Hydrometer	A device for checking specific gravity of liquids. Used to check specific gravity of electrolyte.	**Pendant pedals**	Pedals with levers that are pivoted at the top end.
Hypoid bevel gears	A form of bevel gear used in the rear axle drive gears. The bevel pinion meshes below the centre line of the crownwheel, giving a lower propeller shaft line.	**Phillips screwdriver**	A cross-point screwdriver for use with the cross-slotted heads of Phillips screws.
		Pinion	A small gear, usually in relation to another gear.
Idler	A device for passing on movement. A free running gear between driving and driven gears. A lever transmitting track rod movement to a side rod in steering gear.	**Piston-type damper**	Shock absorber in which damping is controlled by a piston working in a closed oil-filled cylinder.
		Preloading	Preset static pressure on ball or roller bearings not due to working loads.
Impeller	A centrifugal pumping element. Used in water pumps to stimulate flow.	**Radial**	Radiating from a centre, like the spokes of a wheel.

Radius rod	Pivoted arm confining movement of a part to an arc of fixed radius.
Ratchet	Toothed wheel or rack which can move in one direction only, movement in the other being prevented by a pawl.
Ring gear	A gear tooth ring attached to outer periphery of flywheel. Starter pinion engages with it during starting.
Runout	Amount by which rotating part is out of true.
Semi-floating axle	Outer end of rear axle halfshaft is carried on bearing inside axle casing. Wheel hub is secured to end of shaft.
Servo	A hydraulic or pneumatic system for assisting, or, augmenting a physical effort. See 'Vacuum Servo'.
Setscrew	One which is threaded for the full length of the shank.
Shackle	A coupling link, used in the form of two parallel pins connected by side plates to secure the end of the master suspension spring and absorb the effects of deflection.
Shell bearing	Thinwalled steel shell lined with anti-friction metal. Usually semi-circular and used in pairs for main and big-end bearings.
Shock absorber	See 'Damper'.
Silentbloc	Rubber bush bonded to inner and outer metal sleeves.
Socket-head screw	Screw with hexagonal socket for an Allen key.
Solenoid	A coil of wire creating a magnetic field when electric current passes through it. Used with a soft iron core to operate contacts or a mechanical device.
Spur gear	A gear with teeth cut axially across the periphery.
Stub axle	Short axle fixed at one end only.
Tachometer	An instrument for accurate measurement of rotating speed. Usually indicates in revolutions per minute.

TDC	Top Dead Centre. The highest point reached by a piston in a cylinder, with the crank and connecting rod in line.
Thermostat	Automatic device for regulating temperature. Used in vehicle coolant systems to open a valve which restricts circulation at low temperature.
Third motion shaft	Output shaft of gearbox.
Threequarter floating axle	Outer end of rear axle halfshaft flanged and bolted to wheel hub, which runs on bearing mounted on outside of axle casing. Vehicle weight is not carried by the axle shaft.
Thrust bearing or washer	Used to reduce friction in rotating parts subject to axial loads.
Torque	Turning or twisting effort. See 'lb ft'.
Track rod	The bar(s) across the vehicle which connect the steering arms and maintain the front wheels in their correct alignment.
UJ	Universal joint. A coupling between shafts which permits angular movement.
UNF	Unified National Fine screw thread.
Vacuum servo	Device used in brake system, using difference between atmospheric pressure and inlet manifold depression to operate a piston which acts to augment brake pressure as required. See 'Servo'.
Venturi	A restriction or 'choke' in a tube, as in a carburetter, used to increase velocity to obtain a reduction in pressure.
Vernier	A sliding scale for obtaining fractional readings of the graduations of an adjacent scale.
Welch plug	A domed thin metal disc which is partially flattened to lock in a recess. Used to plug core holes in castings.
Wet liner	Removable cylinder barrel, sealed against coolant leakage, where the coolant is in direct contact with the outer surface.
Wet sump	A reservoir attached to the crankcase to hold the lubricating oil.

NOTES

INDEX

NOTES

NOTES